The Reactive Hypoglycemia Miracle Cookbook

Jennifer Winfrey, MA

Contents

Foreword

As a Master's prepared Registered Nurse, I have practiced for over 23 years, and have struggled to find the appropriate diet to assist my patients in keeping their glucose levels at a desirable and consistent level. Even though I have utilized calorie controlled diets that consist of carbohydrate counting, the blood sugar levels of these patients continue to fluctuate. Postprandial hypoglycemia (low blood sugar after a meal) is a common problem for many diabetics and non-diabetics. In many cases, it cannot be attributed to a specific cause. One would think that blood sugar would be exceptionally high immediately after eating. For many, this is not the case.

Postprandial hypoglycemia may occur after a meal as a result of too much insulin being injected by the patient at mealtime and not enough calories being taken in. Or, perhaps the person has fasted for a long period of time, eats a meal, produces too much insulin and the body is not able to metabolize it, thus, resulting in hypoglycemia.

Research conducted on the topic of postprandial hypoglycemia has concluded that in many cases, the person's body is lacking the production of glucagon which is a hormone responsible for maintaining a consistent level of sugar in the blood, again, resulting in postprandial hypoglycemia. This is not just a complication of being a diabetic. Hormonal imbalances caused by pituitary disorders and other disease processes can result in the non-diabetic having episodes of low blood sugar following a meal.

It is my professional opinion that when a person eats they may be eating a meal high in carbohydrates which converts to sugar. This causes the blood sugar to surge high and then plummet quickly resulting in hypoglycemia. It can also be the result of the combinations of food eaten. Whatever the cause, it can be a very dangerous situation.

When our bodies are depleted of the appropriate amount of sugar in our bloodstreams symptoms will be that of nervousness, cold sweating, confusion, rapid heart rate, shortness of breath, dizziness, fatigue and even unconsciousness. This is an extreme emergency and can result in brain damage, cell destruction and even death if not addressed quickly enough and with the appropriate foods that will bring the blood sugar level back to a stable level. Some of the foods that will do this are fruit juices, peanut butter, crackers or instant glucose that can be purchased in tablet or tube form. If the person becomes unconscious it is important to call 911 or get them to the closest emergency department immediately as they will need glucose administered intravenously.

The Reactive Hypoglycemic Miracle Cookbook is one of the best and most well-rounded cookbooks that not only addresses the dietary needs of the diabetic and reactive hypoglycemic, but also provides a variety of palatable recipes for those that must adhere to a gluten-free diet and those that choose to follow a vegan regimen. Packed full of healthy and delicious recipes, this book is the long awaited answer for all. The author suffers from celiac disease so you will see several recipes that are gluten-free. This is a blessing as more and more people are finding that they either have celiac disease or other disease processes that are exacerbated by the consumption of gluten. In addition to promoting better eating habits for the diabetic, the nutritional recipes included in this book include those that are limited in processed foods, red meats and other ingredients that are noted to cause cancer.

This book will also prove to be highly beneficial to the pre-diabetic. Utilizing the provided recipes and adhering to a lifestyle of healthy living can potentially prevent Type II Diabetes from manifesting. Pre-diabetes is a period of time prior to the onset of Diabetes Type II where the blood sugar levels of the patient are either pushing the high normal level around 100 mg/dL of blood or ranging slightly over the high normal cut off with a reading of 100-110 mg/dL of blood. During the pre-diabetes period there is damage being done to the cardiovascular system and the possibility of stroke is heightened.

My plan is to not only use this book personally, but to purchase it for family members and friends. For those patients that I care for, get ready because this book will be a tool that I utilize to teach you about good eating habits that will not only help to get your blood sugar under control after mealtime, but will help to prevent other diseases such as obesity, cardiovascular disease and stroke.

From breakfast to snack time, this book will provide you with recipes for every meal. The recipes can be altered to accommodate parties, brunches and other social gatherings. For your ease, I have included some of the healthier ingredients that are utilized to substitute for those that may be less healthy:

<u>Agave Nectar</u>

Agave nectar is a honey-like sweetener that comes from the agave plant found in south Mexico. This is also the plant that tequila is made from. For hundreds of years agave has been used as a sweetener packed full of nutrients proved to be beneficial to healthy living. For those that do not like the taste of honey, agave offers a much more subtle flavor.

> "One of the most health-promoting properties of agave nectar is its favorable glycemic profile. Its sweetness comes primarily from a complex form of fructose called inulin. Fructose is the sugar that occurs naturally in fruits and vegetables. The carbohydrate in agave nectar has a low glycemic index, which provides sweetness without the unpleasant "sugar rush" and unhealthful blood sugar spike caused by many other sugars. Agave nectar is a delicious natural sweetener that can be used moderately - by dieters, some diabetics, and health conscious cooks - to replace high-glycemic and refined sugars". (All About Agave, 2012)

Bragg's Liquid Aminos. Similar to soy sauce. Great on salads, veggies, dressings, , rice, beans, Wok foods, tofu, gravies, jerky, poultry, fish, popcorn, meats, casseroles, potatoes, etc. Contains important healthy amino acids

In addition, there are a couple of unusual ingredients in one or two recipes:

Xylitol is a low-glycemic sugar alcohol sweetener used as a naturally occurring sugar substitute. It is found in the fibers of many fruits and vegetables.

You can purchase xylitol, agave and Bragg's at natural food stores, Whole Foods, or online at Amazon.com.

Asafoetida has a pungent, unpleasant smell when raw, but in cooked dishes, it delivers a smooth flavor, reminiscent of leeks. It can be purchased in Indian grocery stores.

The Recipes

My intent is to try each and every recipe in this book. Currently, I recommend the potato and cheddar soup which is rich flavored soup with tender cubes of red potato, chunks of ham and the smoky taste of cheddar. This soup, served with a garden salad tossed in balsamic vinegar hits the spot on a cold February afternoon.

Another of my favorites is the black beans and rice. A Mexican staple, the combination of black beans and rice provides a complete protein. Top with chopped lettuce, tomato salsa, and avocado for a filling dish. Sit back and don't worry about a blood sugar emergency.

Recommendation

I recommend that you purchase this book and discover your next step to better health. Remember that the vegan choice is one of the healthiest choices that you can make, however; the author has considered the preferences of all and has provided a variety of choices of delicious recipes to suit the palates of all. Eat to live!

Deanna R. Miller, RN MSN/Ed HCE

References

All about agave, 2012. Health benefits of agave nectar. Retrieved February 8, 2012 from http://www.allaboutagave.com/health-benefits-of-agave-nectar.php

Bragg, 2012. *Bragg liquid aminos*. Retrieved February 8, 2012 from http://bragg.com/products/la.html

Introduction: The Reactive Hypoglycemia Diet

A reactive hypoglycemic diet is different from that of a diabetic or hypoglycemic. High-fiber, restricted-simple sugar, whole grain foods, fruits and vegetables mainly comprise a reactive hypoglycemic diet. However, do not completely avoid carbs because they further aid in blood sugar regulation.

Below is a list of foods to <u>avoid</u> when you have reactive hypoglycemia:

1. Anything that is made from white flour, like white noodles
2. Cereals and other foods that are high in sugar or fructose corn syrup
3. Caffeinated beverages such as coffee, soda and tea
4. Sweet desserts like cakes, muffins and pastries
5. Fatty foods
6. Potato chips
7. Restaurant and fast-food meals (most are packed with unwanted sugar, salt and fat)
8. Alcohol (especially high-sugar alcohols like beer and cider. A glass of dry wine with dinner may actually help with keeping blood sugar stable)

These foods are generally high glycemic, meaning, they are quickly absorbed and processed by your body, which in turn may cause your blood sugar levels to yo-yo. Restaurant and fast-food meals often have hidden sugar and added fats and salts.

Forget the white bread and noodles; go for whole grains. Being complex carbohydrates, whole grain foods are lower on the glycemic index. They are processed more slowly, giving your body time to create a steady flow of glucose. However, eradicate sandwiches, bagels, and other carb-heavy meals from your diet.

For your beverage list, avoid all caffeinated drinks and exchange them with water and non-caffeinated options like herbal teas. Even diet sodas may result in an insulin response, so until you've got your blood sugar under control, it's best to eliminate those as well.

Foods that are high in fat can be replaced with low-calorie, nutritious substitutes like vegan burger, tofu, and fish. Eat them all you can without the guilt and fear of another reactive hypoglycemia attack.
You should, in general, aim for one third protein (in grams) for each meal or snack you eat. However, each body in unique and only you will be able to tell how many carbs you can tolerate without it affecting your blood sugar two or three hours later.

If you like the taste of vinegar, you can also use it a dressing for your salad. Its biochemical action is said to help people with insulin sensitive reactive hypoglycemia.

A person with reactive hypoglycemia should eat every two hours to avoid a crash. You can divide a full meal into two to compensate for this recommended schedule, or supplement your meals with healthful snacks like a lowfat yogurt, a handful of peanuts or a slice of cheese. It is also advisable to drink and eat before engaging into any physical activity.

Finally, make it a habit to read food labels thoroughly to avoid buying the ones that may worsen your condition. Avoid ingredients such as sugar and high fructose syrup.

Why "Miracle"? Eliminating most of the processed foods and simple sugars from your diet, combined with a diet based on plants (using meat and fish in smaller quantities) is the basis for stabilizing your blood sugar and returning you to good health. Give the diet 30 days and I guarantee you'll feel 100 percent better...I did!

How To Use This Book

Start each day with one of the protein-rich breakfasts. Some studies have shown that eating *only* protein for breakfast can help some reactive hypoglycemic sufferers—if this is you, stick to eggs, vegetarian bacon and sausage, or Ezekiel 4:9 toast with peanut butter (you'll find this bread in the freezer section of many grocery stores or in health food stores).

Choose one of the healthful lunch recipes, and continue snacking at least every two hours.

Watch portions carefully. If you begin to gain weight (which, depending on your metabolism is quite possible), reduce portions or up your exercise routine to account for the extra calories.

Try the diet for one month. It will take this long to allow your body to adjust for the extra fiber intake. You may experience headaches or fatigue for the first few days as your body may rebel against the sudden reduction in sugary carbs. *This is temporary.* Once you have rid yourself of sugar and carb cravings—you're symptoms will subside to a more manageable level.

Breakfast

Breakfast Burritos

If you're trying to lose weight, this recipe can be modified. Substitute veggie bacon and low-fat cheese for a lower fat alternative.

1	pound	bacon	8	oz	shredded Cheddar cheese
10		eggs			
1	(16 oz) can	refried beans	10	(10 inch)	whole wheat flour tortillas
			½ cup		salsa

Procedure

1. Place bacon in a large, deep skillet. Cook over medium high heat until evenly brown. Drain, and set aside. Wrap the tortillas in foil and warm in the oven.
2. Fry the eggs in a greased skillet until firm. In a small sauce pan heat the refried beans.
3. Top each tortilla with refried beans, 2 strips of bacon, 1 egg , a little cheese and salsa. Roll tortillas into burritos and serve.

Servings: 10
Yield: 10

Preparation Time: 25 minutes
Total Time: 35 minutes

Nutrition Facts

Serving size: 1/10 of a recipe (6.1 ounces).

Amount Per Serving	
Calories	484.32
Calories From Fat (64%)	310.47
	% Daily Value
Total Fat 34.69g	53%
Saturated Fat 13.59g	68%
Cholesterol 239.5mg	80%
Sodium 885.83mg	37%
Potassium 311.59mg	9%
Total Carbohydrates 21g	7%
Fiber 2.21g	9%
Sugar 1.03g	
Protein 20.93g	42%

Egg and Hash Brown Pie

6	strips	Morningstar veggie bacon, chopped	3	cups	hash brown potatoes, thawed
5		eggs	1/3		chopped green onions
1/2 cup		milk	1 1/2 cup		shredded cheddar cheese, divided

Procedure

1. Place veggie bacon in a large, deep skillet. Cook over medium high heat until evenly brown. Crumble, and set aside.
2. Preheat oven to 350 degrees F (175 degrees C). Lightly grease a 7x11 inch baking dish.
3. In a large bowl, beat together the eggs and milk. Stir in the bacon, hash browns, green onions, and 1 cup shredded Cheddar cheese. Pour into the prepared baking dish.
4. Bake in the preheated oven 25 to 35 minutes, or until a knife inserted in the center comes out clean. Sprinkle the remaining Cheddar cheese on top, and continue baking for 3 to 4 minutes, or until the cheese is melted. Remove from oven, and let sit 5 minutes before serving.

Servings: 8
Yield: 8

Preparation Time: 15 minutes
Cooking Time: 45 minutes
Total Time: 1 hour and 5 minutes

Nutrition Facts

Serving size: 1/8 of a recipe (5.6 ounces).

Amount Per Serving	
Calories	244
Calories From Fat (51%)	124.05
	% Daily Value
Total Fat 13.98g	22%
Saturated Fat 6.27g	31%
Cholesterol 139.96mg	47%
Sodium 376.11mg	16%
Potassium 323.11mg	9%
Total Carbohydrates 16.95g	6%
Fiber 1.73g	7%
Sugar 1.11g	
Protein 12.83g	26%

Irish Eggs

2	Tbsp	olive oil	1	teaspoon	chili powder
2		large potatoes peeled and diced into 1/4" chunks	1		green bell pepper, chopped
1		onion minced	6		eggs beaten
1/2	teaspoon	turmeric			

Procedure

1 In a large skillet, warm olive oil over medium low heat. Add potatoes, onion and green pepper. Cover pan; sauté until potatoes are browned. Stir frequently.

2 Add turmeric and chili powder. Stir well.

3 Push potatoes to one side of pan. Add eggs to pan and then scramble until done. Mix with potatoes and serve.

Servings: 4
Yield: 4

Preparation Time: 15 minutes
Cooking Time: 20 minutes
Total Time: 35 minutes

Nutrition Facts

Serving size: 1/4 of a recipe (8.6 ounces).

Amount Per Serving	
Calories	255.09
Calories From Fat (47%)	118.97
	% Daily Value
Total Fat 13.38g	21%
Saturated Fat 6.11g	31%
Cholesterol 294.27mg	98%
Sodium 148.02mg	6%
Potassium 646.58mg	18%
Total Carbohydrates 22.33g	7%
Fiber 3.91g	16%
Sugar 3.32g	
Protein 12.28g	25%

Mango Smoothie

2 cups yogurt
2 cups chopped fresh mango
1 Tbsp flax seeds

1/2 cup ice
1 Tbsp agave nectar

Procedure

1. Combine all ingredients in a blender and blend until smooth and flax seeds are ground.

Servings: 4
Yield: 4

Preparation Time: 5 minutes

Nutrition Facts

Serving size: 1/4 of a recipe (7.8 ounces).

Amount Per Serving	
Calories	186.08
Calories From Fat (19%)	35.41
	% Daily Value
Total Fat 4.04g	6%
Saturated Fat 0.59g	3%
Cholesterol 0mg	0%
Sodium 19.71mg	<1%
Potassium 293.33mg	8%
Total Carbohydrates 35.51g	12%
Fiber 5.07g	20%
Sugar 22.14g	
Protein 5.46g	11%

Oven Omelet

8		eggs	1	cup	diced cooked ham
1	cup	milk	1	cup	shredded Cheddar cheese
2	cups	shredded hash brown potatoes	1		to taste salt and pepper to taste

Procedure

1 Preheat oven to 350 degrees F (175 degrees C). Lightly grease an 8x8 inch glass baking dish.

2 Beat eggs in a large bowl; stir in the milk. Stir in the potatoes, ham and cheese. Season to taste and pour into prepared pan.

3 Bake in preheated oven for 45 to 50, until knife inserted in middle comes out clean.

Servings: 7
Yield: 6-8

Preparation Time: 5 minutes
Cooking Time: 45 minutes
Total Time: 50 minutes

Nutrition Facts

Serving size: 1/7 of a recipe (6.6 ounces).

Amount Per Serving	
Calories	226.37
Calories From Fat (48%)	109.03
	% Daily Value
Total Fat 12.26g	19%
Saturated Fat 5.85g	29%
Cholesterol 238.17mg	79%
Sodium 326.5mg	14%
Potassium 355.16mg	10%
Total Carbohydrates 13.73g	5%
Fiber 0.98g	4%
Sugar 2.63g	
Protein 15.1g	30%

American Scramble

Think tofu is bland? You'll be surprised by this recipe, which resembles scrambled eggs but has a greatly reduced amount of cholesterol.

2	Tbsp	olive oil	1	Tbsp	nutritional yeast
1		green bell pepper, seeded and chopped	1	tsp	turmeric
			1/2 tsp		freshly ground black pepper
1	small	onion chopped			
1/2 cup		sliced mushrooms	4	slices	American cheese slices
12	oz	extra-firm tofu, drained and pressed			

Procedure

1. Heat 2T olive oil in a saucepan over medium heat. Add the onion, pepper and mushroom. Sauté for 4-5 minutes until onion is translucent.
2. Add the tofu and then stir often for 5 to 7 min. Add the nutritional yeast, turmeric, and black pepper and stir well.
3. Top with cheese.

Servings: 4
Yield: 4

Preparation Time: 15 minutes
Cooking Time: 10 minutes

Nutrition Facts

Serving size: 1/4 of a recipe (6.9 ounces).

Amount Per Serving	
Calories	255.17
Calories From Fat (65%)	165.93
	% Daily Value
Total Fat 19.11g	29%
Saturated Fat 5.98g	30%
Cholesterol 18.7mg	6%
Sodium 466.89mg	19%
Potassium 339.19mg	10%
Total Carbohydrates 8.9g	3%
Fiber 1.56g	6%
Sugar 4.78g	
Protein 14.94g	30%

Oven Scrambled Eggs

An easy way to cook scrambled eggs for a crowd.

1/2 cup	margarine, melted		2 1/4 tsp	salt
24	eggs		2 1/2 cup	milk

Procedure

1 Preheat the oven to 350 degrees F (175 degrees C).
2 Pour melted butter into a glass 9x13 inch baking dish. In a large bowl, whisk together eggs and salt until well blended. Gradually whisk in milk. Pour egg mixture into the baking dish.
3 Bake uncovered for 10 minutes, then stir, and bake an additional 10 to 15 minutes, or until eggs are set. Serve immediately.

Servings: 12
Yield: 12

Preparation Time: 10 minutes
Cooking Time: 25 minutes
Total Time: 35 minutes

Nutrition Facts

Serving size: 1/12 of a recipe (5.7 ounces).

Amount Per Serving	
Calories	236
Calories From Fat (68%)	161.58
	% Daily Value
Total Fat 18.08g	28%
Saturated Fat 5.08g	25%
Cholesterol 376.07mg	125%
Sodium 690.56mg	29%
Potassium 213.2mg	6%
Total Carbohydrates 3.24g	1%
Fiber 0g	0%
Sugar 2.94g	
Protein 14.32g	29%

Sausage Egg Squares

As a vegetarian alternative, use Morningstar farm sausage links instead of regular sausage.

1	pound	turkey Italian sausage links, casings removed	1 1/2	cup		egg substitute
1		medium green pepper chopped	1	cup		fat free milk
1	small	onion chopped	1	cup		Pamela's Gluten-free baking mix
1	(16 oz)	package small curd 1% cottage cheese	1	(4 ounce) can		chopped green chilies
2	cups	shredded reduced fat Cheddar cheese				

Procedure

1. In a large nonstick skillet, cook sausage, green pepper and onion over medium heat until meat is no longer pink; drain. Stir in the remaining ingredients. Pour into a 13-in. x 9-in. x 2-in. baking dish coated with nonstick cooking spray. Bake at 350 degrees F for 35-40 minutes or until a knife inserted near the center comes out clean. Let stand for 10 minutes before cutting.

Preparation Time: 15 minutes
Cooking Time: 35 minutes
Total Time: 50 minutes

Nutrition Facts

Serving size: Entire recipe (75.6 ounces).

Amount Per Serving	
Calories	2890.12
Calories From Fat (48%)	1383.66
	% Daily Value
Total Fat 156.27g	240%
Saturated Fat 72.36g	362%
Cholesterol 638.62mg	213%
Sodium 8096.16mg	337%
Potassium 4168.44mg	119%
Total Carbohydrates 130.67g	44%
Fiber 6.18g	25%
Sugar 39.37g	
Protein 233.25g	467%

Spanish-Style Scrambler Wrap

Similar to the breakfast burrito recipe, this uses tofu instead of eggs. The consistency is similar to eggs when cooked and is a delicious alternative to high cholesterol eggs.

2	Tbsp	olive oil	1	tsp	ground cumin
1	cup	red and green bell pepper, chopped	1	tsp	turmeric
1	small	onion chopped	1	pound	fresh spinach
12	oz	extra-firm tofu, crumbled	1/2	cup	salsa
1/2	cup	low-sodium vegetable broth	4	(8 inch)	whole wheat tortillas
1	tsp	chili powder			

Procedure

1 Heat olive oil over medium heat in a skillet. Add the bell pepper and onion and sauté until onion is translucent.
2 Add the tofu, 1/4 cup broth, chili powder, cumin and turmeric. Sauté stirring often, for 5 to 7 min, or until lightly brown. Add spinach and remaining 1/4 cup broth and cook 1 min until spinach has wilted.
3 Add salsa and stir.
4 Divide the tofu mixture evenly among the tortillas and roll up the filling.

Servings: 4
Yield: 4

Preparation Time: 5 minutes
Cooking Time: 22 minutes

Nutrition Facts

Serving size: 1/4 of a recipe (15 ounces).

Amount Per Serving	
Calories	224.73
Calories From Fat (52%)	116.89
	% Daily Value
Total Fat 13.57g	21%
Saturated Fat 1.62g	8%
Cholesterol 0.31mg	<1%
Sodium 783.54mg	33%
Potassium 724.71mg	21%
Total Carbohydrates 16.7g	6%
Fiber 6.77g	27%
Sugar 3.69g	
Protein 14.93g	30%

Spinach Frittata

1/3 cup	vegetable broth	
2	medium	potatoes peeled and chopped into 1/4-inch cubes
2		garlic cloves, minced

1	bag	spinach, washed
1/4 cup		cream or milk
16	oz	extra-firm tofu, crumbled
1/8 tsp		turmeric
1/8 tsp		salt
1/4 tsp		freshly ground black pepper
1/4 tsp		chili powder

Procedure

1. Add broth, potatoes and garlic to a medium pan. Cover pan. Bring to a boil and then simmer on low until potatoes are soft, about 15 minutes. Stir once every five minutes. Add spinach and sauté until spinach is wilted.

2. Preheat the oven to 375 degrees F while the potatoes and garlic are cooking.

3. Puree half the tofu with cream or milk, turmeric, salt, black pepper and chili powder in a food processor. Crumble the other half. Combine pureed tofu, remaining crumbled tofu, and spinach mixture in a 6x6-inch baking dish and mix thoroughly. Bake for 20 min. Remove from the oven and allow it to set for at least 10 min before serving.

Servings: 8
Yield: 8

Preparation Time: 10 minutes
Cooking Time: 20 minutes

Nutrition Facts

Serving size: 1/8 of a recipe (6.5 ounces).

Amount Per Serving	
Calories	113.92
Calories From Fat (28%)	31.38
	% Daily Value
Total Fat 3.75g	6%
Saturated Fat 0.4g	2%
Cholesterol 0.1mg	<1%
Sodium 157.39mg	7%
Potassium 637.07mg	18%
Total Carbohydrates 13.92g	5%
Fiber 2.83g	11%
Sugar 0.95g	
Protein 8.62g	17%

Sweet Potato Hash

Sweet potatoes are lower on the glycemic index than regular potatoes. Try this sweet potato dish as an alternative to regular hash.

2	pounds	sweet potatoes peeled and cut into 1/2-inch pieces
2 tbsp		olive oil
3		garlic cloves, chopped
1		small onion chopped
1		small red bell pepper, chopped
1		small green bell pepper, chopped

1	Tbsp	sweet paprika
		kosher or sea salt to taste
		Freshly ground black pepper to taste
6		eggs beaten
2	Tbsp	olive oil

Procedure

1. Place sweet potatoes with water to cover in a large saucepan. Simmer potatoes for about 15 to 17 min until just tender. Drain and set aside.
2. Heat oil in a large skillet over medium heat. Cook garlic, onion and bell peppers for about 4 min. Add paprika, salt and black pepper and continue to cook for 5 min. until vegetable are soft. Add the sweet potatoes and cook to heat through.
3. Heat a separate pan over medium heat and scramble the eggs in the olive oil. Combine all ingredients.

Servings: 6
Yield: 6

Preparation Time: 15 minutes
Cooking Time: 35 minutes

Nutrition Facts

Serving size: 1/6 of a recipe (10.1 ounces).

Amount Per Serving	
Calories	274.33
Calories From Fat (32%)	87.17
	% Daily Value
Total Fat 9.78g	15%
Saturated Fat 2.3g	12%
Cholesterol 186.1mg	62%
Sodium 272.56mg	11%
Potassium 751.42mg	21%
Total Carbohydrates 37.55g	13%
Fiber 6.4g	26%
Sugar 9.1g	
Protein 9.84g	20%

Fruit And Granola Parfait

1/2 cup	granola	1/4 tsp	ground cardamom
3/4 cup	vanilla yogurt	1/4 cup	fresh berries
1/2 tsp	agave nectar	2	brazil nuts, crushed

Procedure

1 Divide granola into 2 parfait glasses.
2 In a small bowl, mix together the yogurt, agave nectar and cardamom. Spoon this onto the granola.
3 Top the yogurt with berries.
4 Scatter the Brazil nuts on top of Berries.

Servings: 2
Yield: 2

Preparation Time: 5 minutes

Nutrition Facts

Serving size: 1/2 of a recipe (5 ounces).

Amount Per Serving	
Calories	182.73
Calories From Fat (35%)	63.62
	% Daily Value
Total Fat 7.41g	11%
Saturated Fat 1.28g	6%
Cholesterol 0mg	0%
Sodium 34.57mg	1%
Potassium 93.47mg	3%
Total Carbohydrates 26.24g	9%
Fiber 2.06g	8%
Sugar 15.83g	
Protein 4.72g	9%

Dinner

Chicken and More

Egg Fried Rice

Think you can't eat fried rice again? Think again! My son swears this tastes better than the fried rice from our local Chinese restaurant. Make sure to use dark sesame oil for the best flavor. Vegetarians can use Quorn instead of chicken.

4	cups	cooked Texmati Rice Select light brown rice	1		yellow pepper chopped
4	Tbsp	sesame oil	1	cup	snow peas
4		chicken breasts	1	cup	peas
1		onion chopped	8	Tbsp	Bragg's liquid aminos
1		red pepper chopped	2		eggs beaten

Procedure

1. chop chicken breasts into small chunks
2. brown over medium heat
3. add onion and cook 3-4 minutes until onions are softened
4. add remaining vegetables and stir fry 3 minutes
5. add rice and Bragg's. Stir fry until all ingredients are combined well -- no more than 1-2 minutes
6. Push rice to side of pan. Add eggs, scramble and then combine with rice.

Servings: 4
Yield: 4

Degree of Difficulty: Easy

Cooking Time: 15 minutes
Total Time: 15 minutes

Nutrition Facts

Serving size: 1/4 of a recipe (29 ounces).

Amount Per Serving	
Calories	896.95
Calories From Fat (23%)	204.36
	% Daily Value
Total Fat 22.3g	34%
Total Carbohydrates 99.09g	33%
Protein 70.96g	142%

Jacksonville Fried Chicken

1	tsp	salt	3	Tbsp	yellow mustard
1/2	tsp	onion powder	1/2	cup	water
1	tsp	pepper	2	Tbsp	baking powder
1	tsp	garlic powder	4		chicken breasts
2	cups	Pamela's Gluten-free baking mix			vegetable oil for frying, heated to 375 degrees

Procedure

1 mix salt, onion, pepper, garlic powder and baking mix in a large bowl

2 dilute mustard with 1/2 cup water

3 add 1/3 cup baking mix to mustard

4 add baking powder to remaining dry baking mixture

5 dip chunks into mustard mix, then into baking mix.

6 fry until golden brown, about 5 minutes

Serve with chili fries (see recipe)

Servings: 4
Yield: 4

Nutrition Facts

Serving size: 1/4 of a recipe (12 ounces).

Amount Per Serving	
Calories	515.51
Calories From Fat (29%)	147.4
	% Daily Value
Total Fat 16.46g	25%
Saturated Fat 3.44g	17%
Cholesterol 151.04mg	50%
Sodium 2426.26mg	101%
Potassium 972.35mg	28%
Total Carbohydrates 34.94g	12%
Fiber 4.2g	17%
Sugar 0.14g	
Protein 55.06g	110%

Seasoned Chili fries

1	Tbsp olive oil	1/2 tsp	chili powder
1/2 tsp	paprika	1/2 tsp	onion
1/2 tsp	garlic powder		

Procedure

1. Slice potatoes thinly, about 1/4 inch in diameter
2. Combine ingredients in a large freezer bag and shake well
3. Spread on a cookie sheet and bake at 450 degrees for 20-25 minutes, until slightly blackened at the edges.

Servings: 1
Yield: 1

Nutrition Facts

Serving size:
Entire recipe
(0.8 ounces).

Amount Per Serving	
Calories	133.52
Calories From Fat (92%)	122.33
	% Daily Value
Total Fat 13.86g	21%
Saturated Fat 1.93g	10%
Cholesterol 0mg	0%
Sodium 24.32mg	1%
Potassium 78.47mg	2%
Total Carbohydrates 2.89g	<1%
Fiber 1.1g	4%
Sugar 0.47g	
Protein 0.66g	1%

Recipe Tips

Serve a small portion (about 1/2 potato) with a healthy protein portion and a side of vegetables for a complete meal. Ingredients listed are per potato.

Author Notes

Think you can't eat fries if you have reactive hypoglycemia? Not true! Moderation is the key.

Boneless Buffalo Wings

Depriving yourself of comfort food is a recipe for disaster. My family -- two of us with reactive hypoglycemia -- treat ourselves to a fried meal once a month. As a vegetarian alternative, try Quorn chik'n chunks for great popcorn chicken.

	oil for deep frying	1			egg
1	cup	Pamela's Gluten-free	3/4	cup	milk
		baking mix	3		skinless,
1/2	tsp	ground black pepper			boneless
1/2	tsp	cayenne pepper			chicken breasts,
1/4	tsp	garlic powder			cut into 1/2
1/2	tsp	paprika			inch strips
			1/4	cup	hot pepper sauce
			1	Tbsp	butter

Procedure

1. Heat oil in a deep-fryer or large saucepan to 375 degrees F (190 degrees C).
2. Combine Pamela's baking mix, black pepper, cayenne pepper, garlic powder, and paprika in a large bowl. Whisk together the egg and milk in a small bowl. Dip each piece of chicken in the egg mixture, and then roll in the flour blend. Repeat so that each piece of chicken is double coated. Refrigerate breaded chicken for 20 minutes.
3. Fry chicken in the hot oil, in batches. Cook until the exterior is nicely browned and the juices run clear, 5 to 6 minutes a batch.
4. Combine hot sauce and butter in a small bowl. Microwave sauce on High until melted, 20 to 30 seconds. Pour sauce over the cooked chicken; mix to coat.

Servings: 3
Yield: 3

Preparation Time: 10 minutes
Cooking Time: 20 minutes
Total Time: 50 minutes

Nutrition Facts

Serving size: 1/3 of a recipe (10.8 ounces).

Amount Per Serving	
Calories	1060.15
Calories From Fat (72%)	763.34
	% Daily Value
Total Fat 86.3g	133%
Saturated Fat 11.93g	60%
Cholesterol 146.5mg	49%
Sodium 611.94mg	25%
Potassium 434.06mg	12%
Total Carbohydrates 36.07g	12%
Fiber 1.51g	6%
Sugar 3.61g	
Protein 35.44g	71%

Chicken Cordon Bleu

This makes for a great special occasion dinner. For a vegetarian alternative, use Quorn chik'n patties instead of chicken. If using Quorn, place the filling between two patties and then dip in water before coating.

6		skinless, boneless chicken breast halves	6	Tbsp	olive oil
6		slices Swiss cheese	1/2	cup	dry white wine
6		slices ham or vegetarian ham	1	tsp	chicken bouillon granules or vegan bouillon granules
3	Tbsp	Pamela's Gluten-free baking mix	1	Tbsp	corn starch
1	tsp	paprika	1/4	cup	heavy (whipping) cream

Procedure

1 Pound chicken breasts if they are too thick. Place a cheese and ham slice on each breast within 1/2 inch of the edges. Fold the edges of the chicken over the filling, and secure with toothpicks. Mix the baking mix and paprika in a small bowl, and roll the chicken pieces in the baking mix.

2 Heat the olive oil in a large skillet over medium heat, and cook the chicken until browned on all sides. Add the wine and bouillon. Reduce heat to low, cover, and simmer for 30 minutes, until chicken is no longer pink and juices run clear.

3 Remove the toothpicks, and transfer the breasts to a warm platter. Blend the cornstarch with the cream in a small bowl, and whisk slowly into the skillet. Cook, stirring until thickened, and drizzle over the chicken. Serve warm.

Servings: 6
Yield: 6

Preparation Time: 15 minutes
Cooking Time: 45 minutes
Total Time: 1 hour

Nutrition Facts

Serving size: 1/6 of a recipe (12.7 ounces).

Amount Per Serving	
Calories	638.01
Calories From Fat (53%)	335.69
	% Daily Value
Total Fat 37.99g	58%
Saturated Fat 20.9g	105%
Cholesterol 270.28mg	90%
Sodium 717.71mg	30%
Potassium 1027.65mg	29%
Total Carbohydrates 7.48g	2%
Fiber 0.31g	1%
Sugar 0.95g	
Protein 60.59g	121%

Chicken Noodle Casserole

Vegetarians can replace the chicken in this comfort meal with Quorn chunks.

4	skinless, boneless chicken breast halves	1/2 tsp	thyme
		1 pinch	salt
		1 pinch	ground black pepper
1 Tbsp	olive oil	½ t	red pepper flakes
2	garlic cloves, minced	1 1/2 cup	crumbled buttery round crackers
1/2	onion chopped		butter-flavored spray
2	celery sticks, chopped		
12 oz	whole wheat egg noodles		
1 (10.75 oz) can	condensed cream of mushroom soup		
1 (10.75 oz) jar	white pasta sauce		
12 oz	frozen broccoli, chopped		

Procedure

1 Poach chicken in a large pot of simmering water. Cook until no longer pink in center, about 12 minutes. Remove from pot and set aside. Bring chicken cooking water to a boil and cook pasta in it according to time indicated on pasta directions. Drain. Cut chicken into small pieces, and mix with noodles.

2 Sauté garlic and onion in a skillet until almost translucent, about three minutes. Add celery and cook for two more minutes.

3 In a separate bowl, mix together mushroom soup, pasta sauce, thyme, and red pepper. Season with salt and pepper. Gently stir all

ingredients together, except for the crackers and butter-flavored spray. Place in a 2 quart baking dish.

4 Spray crumbled crackers with several squirts of butter flavored spray. Top casserole with the buttery crackers.

5 Bake at 350 degrees F (175 degrees C) for about 30 minutes, until heated through and browned on top.

Servings: 6
Yield: 6

Preparation Time: 30 minutes
Cooking Time: 30 minutes
Total Time: 1 hour

Nutrition Facts

Serving size: 1/6 of a recipe (13.2 ounces).

Amount Per Serving	
Calories	538.59
Calories From Fat (35%)	190.23
	% Daily Value
Total Fat 21.48g	33%
Saturated Fat 7.58g	38%
Cholesterol 128.82mg	43%
Sodium 744.52mg	31%
Potassium 650.46mg	19%
Total Carbohydrates 53.3g	18%
Fiber 3.59g	14%
Sugar 3.38g	
Protein 32.87g	66%

Chicken Curry

Serve with brown basmati rice for an authentic Sri Lankan dish.

3	(6 oz)	boneless, skinless chicken breast	6	whole	cloves
			12		curry leaves
2	Tbsp	white vinegar	1	tsp	fresh ginger root, crushed
1	tsp	tamarind juice (optional)	1	(2 inch)	cinnamon stick, broken in half
1/4 cup		Madras curry powder			
1	Tbsp	salt or to taste	3		cloves garlic minced
1	tsp	ground black pepper			
2	Tbsp	coconut oil	1/2	cup	water
1		red onion sliced	1 1/2	Tbsp	tomato paste
4		green Chili peppers halved lengthwise	3	Tbsp	roasted Madras curry powder
8		green cardamom pods			
			1/2	(14 oz) can	coconut milk

Procedure

1 Cut the chicken into bite-sized pieces. Combine the vinegar, tamarind juice, 1/4 cup curry powder, salt, and pepper in a bowl. Add chicken and toss to coat.

2 Heat the coconut oil in a wok or frying pan over medium heat. Cook the sliced onion, green chilies, cardamom pods, cloves, curry leaves, ginger, and cinnamon stick until the onion has softened and turned translucent, about 5 minutes. Reduce heat to medium-low, and continue cooking and stirring until the onion is very tender and dark brown, 15 to 20 minutes more. Stir in the garlic and cook for an additional minute.

3 Add the chicken mixture, water, and tomato paste. Stir and simmer until the chicken is cooked through, about 10 minutes. Add the roasted curry powder and stir until evenly dispersed.

4 Gradually stir in the coconut milk and simmer for 2-3 more minutes. (Do not overheat or the coconut milk may curdle.)

Servings: 4

Yield: 4

Preparation Time: 25 minutes
Cooking Time: 35 minutes
Total Time: 1 hour

Nutrition Facts

Serving size: 1/4 of a recipe (9.9 ounces).

Amount Per Serving	
Calories	437.58
Calories From Fat (46%)	201.76
	% Daily Value
Total Fat 23.42g	36%
Saturated Fat 14.36g	72%
Cholesterol 89.25mg	30%
Sodium 1375.34mg	57%
Potassium 777.53mg	22%
Total Carbohydrates 24.16g	8%
Fiber 5.88g	24%
Sugar 3.33g	
Protein 36.78g	74%

Sweet and Spicy Stir Fry with Chicken and Broccoli

Serve this dish-with-a-kick over brown jasmine rice.

3	cups	broccoli florets	1	Tbsp	Bragg's liquid aminos
1	Tbsp	olive oil	1/2 tsp		ground ginger
2		skinless, boneless chicken breast halves cut into 1 inch strips	1/4 tsp		crushed red pepper
			1/2 tsp		salt
			1/2 tsp		black pepper
1/4 cup		sliced green onions	1/8 cup		chicken stock
1	Tbsp	hoisin sauce			
1	Tbsp	Chili paste			

Procedure

1. Place broccoli in a steamer over 1 inch of boiling water, and cover. Cook until tender but still firm, about 5 minutes.
2. Heat the oil in a skillet over medium heat, and sauté the chicken, green onions, and garlic until the chicken is no longer pink and juices run clear.
3. Stir the hoisin sauce, Chili paste, and Bragg's into the skillet. Add ginger, red pepper, salt, and black pepper. Stir in the chicken stock and simmer about 2 minutes. Mix in the steamed broccoli until coated with the sauce mixture.

Servings: 4
Yield: 4

Preparation Time: 10 minutes
Cooking Time: 20 minutes
Total Time: 30 minutes

Nutrition Facts

Serving size: 1/4 of a recipe (4.7 ounces).

Amount Per Serving	
Calories	139.61
Calories From Fat (34%)	47.31
	% Daily Value
Total Fat 5.33g	8%
Saturated Fat 0.98g	5%
Cholesterol 36.67mg	12%
Sodium 559.93mg	23%
Potassium 347.48mg	10%
Total Carbohydrates 7.58g	3%
Fiber 0.5g	2%
Sugar 1.39g	
Protein 15.94g	32%

Brazilian Black Bean Stew

1	Tbsp	canola oil	2	(14.5 oz) can	diced tomatoes with juice
1/4	pound	chorizo sausage, chopped			
1/3	pound	cooked ham, chopped	1	small	hot green chili pepper diced
1	medium	onion, chopped			
2		clove garlic minced	1 1/2	cup	water
			2	(16 oz) can	black beans rinsed and drained
2	(1 pound)	sweet potatoes peeled and diced			
1	large	red bell pepper, diced	1		mango peeled, seeded and diced
			1/4	cup	chopped fresh cilantro
			1/4	tsp	salt

Procedure

1 Heat the oil in a large pot over medium heat, and cook the chorizo and ham 2 to 3 minutes. Place the onion in the pot, and cook until tender. Stir in garlic, and cook until tender, then mix in the sweet potatoes, bell pepper, tomatoes with juice, chili pepper, and water. Bring to a boil, reduce heat to low, cover, and simmer 15 minutes, until sweet potatoes are tender.

2 Stir the beans into the pot, and cook uncovered until heated through. Mix in the mango and cilantro, and season with salt.

Servings: 6
Yield: 6

Preparation Time: 15 minutes
Cooking Time: 30 minutes
Total Time: 45 minutes

Amount Per Serving	
Calories	358.97
Calories From Fat (31%)	112.25
	% Daily Value
Total Fat 12.36g	19%
Saturated Fat 3.73g	19%
Cholesterol 34.03mg	11%
Sodium 1355.27mg	56%
Potassium 1279.33mg	37%
Total Carbohydrates 44.52g	15%
Fiber 8.16g	33%
Sugar 10.71g	
Protein 19.06g	38%

Burrito Pie

1	pounds	ground beef or tofu crumbles	1/2 (10 oz) can		diced tomatoes with habanero
1		onion chopped			chili peppers
1	tsp	minced garlic	1	(16 oz) jar	Taco Bell hot
6	Tbsp	black olives, sliced			restaurant sauce
			1	(16 oz) can	refried beans
1/2 (4 oz) can		diced green chili peppers	6	(8 inch)	flour tortillas
			4.5	oz	shredded Colby cheese

Procedure

1. Preheat oven to 350 degrees F (175 degrees C).
2. In a large skillet over medium heat, sauté the ground beef for 5 minutes. Add the onion and garlic, and sauté for 5 more minutes. Drain any excess fat, if desired. Mix in the olives, green chili peppers, tomatoes with green chili peppers, taco sauce and refried beans. Stir mixture thoroughly, reduce heat to low, and let simmer for 15 to 20 minutes.
3. Spread a thin layer of the meat mixture in the bottom of a 4 quart casserole dish. Cover with a layer of tortillas spread with refried beans, followed by more meat mixture, then a layer of cheese. Repeat tortilla/bean, meat, cheese pattern until all the tortillas are used, topping off with a layer of meat mixture and cheese.
4. Bake for 20 to 30 minutes in the preheated oven, or until cheese is slightly brown and bubbly.

Servings: 8
Yield: 1 pie

Preparation Time: 30 minutes
Cooking Time: 30 minutes
Total Time: 1 hour

Nutrition Facts

Serving size: 1/8 of a recipe (6.1 ounces).

Amount Per Serving	
Calories	283.83
Calories From Fat (44%)	124.41
	% Daily Value
Total Fat 13.69g	21%
Saturated Fat 5.22g	26%
Cholesterol 42.47mg	14%
Sodium 606.51mg	25%
Potassium 340.94mg	10%
Total Carbohydrates 20.99g	7%
Fiber 2.85g	11%
Sugar 2.11g	
Protein 18.37g	37%

Fish

Baked Halibut

1	tsp	olive oil	2	Tbsp	chopped fresh basil
1	cup	diced zucchini	1/4	tsp	salt
1/2	cup	minced onion	1/4	tsp	ground black pepper
1	clove	garlic peeled and minced	4	(6 oz)	halibut steaks
2	cups	diced fresh tomatoes	1/3	cup	crumbled feta cheese

Procedure

1. Preheat oven to 450 degrees F (230 degrees C). Lightly grease a shallow baking dish.
2. Heat olive oil in a medium saucepan over medium heat and stir in zucchini, onion, and garlic. Cook and stir 5 minutes or until tender. Remove saucepan from heat and mix in tomatoes, basil, salt, and pepper.
3. Arrange halibut steaks in a single layer in the prepared baking dish. Spoon equal amounts of the zucchini mixture over each steak. Top with feta cheese.
4. Bake 15 minutes in the preheated oven, or until fish is easily flaked with a fork.

Servings: 4
Yield: 4

Preparation Time: 15 minutes
Cooking Time: 15 minutes
Total Time: 30 minutes

Nutrition Facts

Serving size: 1/4 of a recipe (12.6 ounces).

Amount Per Serving	
Calories	344.39
Calories From Fat (41%)	141.09
	% Daily Value
Total Fat 15.78g	**24%**
Saturated Fat 3.93g	**20%**
Cholesterol 129.91mg	**43%**
Sodium 395.35mg	**16%**
Potassium 1022.78mg	**29%**
Total Carbohydrates 8.25g	**3%**
Fiber 2.63g	**11%**
Sugar 4.55g	
Protein 41.54g	**83%**

Blackened Tuna Steaks

2	Tbsp	olive oil	1 1/2 tsp		olive oil
2	Tbsp	lime juice	2	Tbsp	paprika
2		Cloves garlic minced	1	Tbsp	cayenne pepper
4		tuna steaks	1	Tbsp	onion powder
1		fresh mango peeled, pitted and chopped	2	tsp	salt
			1	tsp	ground black pepper
1/4 cup		finely chopped red bell pepper	1	tsp	dried thyme
			1	tsp	dried basil
1/2		Spanish onion, finely chopped	1	tsp	dried oregano
1		green onion chopped	1	Tbsp	garlic powder
2	Tbsp	chopped fresh cilantro	4	Tbsp	olive oil
1		Jalapeno pepper seeded and minced			
2	Tbsp	lime juice			

Procedure

1 Whisk together the olive oil, lime juice, and garlic in a bowl. Rub the tuna steaks with the mixture. Place the steaks in a sealable container and chill in refrigerator 3 hours.

2 Combine the mango, bell pepper, Spanish onion, green onion, cilantro, and jalapeno pepper in a bowl; stir. Add the lime juice and 1 1/2 teaspoons olive oil and toss to combine. Chill in refrigerator 1 hour.

3 Stir together the paprika, cayenne pepper, onion powder, salt, pepper, thyme, basil, oregano, and garlic powder in a bowl. Remove the tuna steaks from the refrigerator and gently rinse with water and then dip each side of each steak in the spice mixture to coat.

4 Heat 2 tablespoons olive oil in a large skillet over medium heat. Gently lay the tuna steaks into the hot oil. Cook the tuna on one side for 3 minutes; remove to a plate. Pour the remaining 2 tablespoons olive oil into the skillet and let it get hot. Lay the tuna with the uncooked side down into the skillet and cook another 3 minutes; remove from heat immediately.

5 Spoon about 1/2 cup of the mango salsa onto each of 4 plates. Lay the tuna steaks atop the salsa and serve immediately.

Servings: 4
Yield: 4

Preparation Time: 45 minutes
Cooking Time: 10 minutes
Total Time: 3 hours and 55 minutes

Nutrition Facts

Serving size: 1/4 of a recipe (5.4 ounces).

Amount Per Serving	
Calories	298.08
Calories From Fat (71%)	212.04
	% Daily Value
Total Fat 24.02g	37%
Saturated Fat 3.51g	18%
Cholesterol 8.08mg	3%
Sodium 1180.88mg	49%
Potassium 382.67mg	11%
Total Carbohydrates 17.21g	6%
Fiber 3.89g	16%
Sugar 8.51g	
Protein 7.17g	14%

Bayou Blend

4 Tbsp	Butter or Margarine, divided	1	(4.5 oz) jar	sliced mushrooms, drained
1 large	onion chopped	1	tsp	garlic salt
2	celery ribs, chopped	3/4 tsp		hot pepper sauce
1 large	green pepper chopped	1/2 tsp		cayenne pepper
1 pound	cooked medium shrimp, peeled and deveined	3/4 cup		cooked rice
		3/4 cup		shredded Cheddar cheese
2 (6 oz) cans	crab meat, drained, flaked and cartilage removed	1/2 cup		crushed butter-flavored crackers
1 (10.75 oz) can	condensed cream of mushroom soup, undiluted			
1 (10.75 oz) can	tomatoes, diced			

Procedure

1. In a large skillet, sauté the onion, celery and green pepper in butter until tender. Stir in the shrimp, crab, soup, mushrooms, tomatoes garlic salt, hot pepper sauce, cayenne and rice.
2. Transfer to a greased 2-qt. baking dish. Combine cheese and cracker crumbs; sprinkle over the top. Bake, uncovered, at 350 degrees F for 25-30 minutes or until bubbly.

Servings: 6
Yield: 6

Preparation Time: 20 minutes
Cooking Time: 25 minutes

Total Time: 45 minutes

Nutrition Facts

Serving size: 1/6 of a recipe (10.8 ounces).

Amount Per Serving	
Calories	435.63
Calories From Fat (58%)	252.67
	% Daily Value
Total Fat 28.7g	44%
Saturated Fat 15.73g	79%
Cholesterol 250.1mg	83%
Sodium 1556.73mg	65%
Potassium 472.46mg	13%
Total Carbohydrates 15.38g	5%
Fiber 2.38g	10%
Sugar 4.12g	
Protein 29.13g	58%

Curry Shrimp Au Gratin

1 1/2	cup	brown rice
3	cups	water
6	Tbsp	olive oil
1/4	cup	chopped red bell and green bell pepper
1/2	cup	chopped onion
1/2	cup	chopped celery
1		can mushrooms
3	Tbsp	Tapioca flour
1	tsp	garlic salt
1	cup	peas, drained
3	tsp	curry powder
2	cups	milk
1/2	tsp	agave nectar
2	Tbsp	lime juice
1	cup	shredded mild cheddar cheese, divided
1	pound	shelled, deveined cooked shrimp
1	pinch	Paprika, or more to taste

Procedure

1. Cook rice according to package directions.
2. Preheat oven to 375 degrees F (190 degrees C). Grease a 2-quart baking dish.
3. Place olive oil in a large saucepan, and cook the onion, peppers and celery over medium heat until tender, about 10 minutes, stirring occasionally. Add the peas and mushrooms. Stir in the flour, garlic salt, and curry powder until smooth; let cook for a minute or two. Gradually whisk in the milk, and bring almost to a boil, whisking constantly until thickened, about 5 minutes. Remove from heat, and stir in agave, lime juice, and 1/2 cup of Cheddar cheese; whisk until the cheese melts and the sauce is smooth.
4. Spread the cooked rice out into the prepared baking dish, and top with the cooked shrimp in an even layer. Cover the shrimp with the cheese sauce; push the tines of a fork all over the casserole between the shrimp to allow the sauce to soak into the rice. Top the casserole with the remaining Cheddar cheese, and garnish with paprika.
5. Bake in the preheated oven until bubbly and browned, about 30 minutes.

Servings: 6
Yield: 6

Preparation Time: 20 minutes
Cooking Time: 55 minutes
Total Time: 1 hour and 15 minutes

Nutrition Facts

Serving size: 1/6 of a recipe (14.9 ounces).

Amount Per Serving	
Calories	487.48
Calories From Fat (37%)	182.51
	% Daily Value
Total Fat 20.73g	**32%**
Saturated Fat 12.51g	**63%**
Cholesterol 152.07mg	**51%**
Sodium 986.53mg	**41%**
Potassium 381.65mg	**11%**
Total Carbohydrates 51.78g	**17%**
Fiber 1.67g	**7%**
Sugar 6.14g	
Protein 22.63g	**45%**

Easy Cod Chowder

1	(14.5 oz) can	diced tomatoes	1 tsp	dried basil
3	stalks	celery chopped		salt and pepper to taste
1	tsp	dried oregano		
			1/2 pound	frozen cod fillets

Procedure

1. In a medium sized stock pot place tomatoes, celery, oregano, basil, salt and pepper. Bring to a boil over medium heat.

2. Place frozen fish filets in pot. Reduce heat and cook for 10 to 15 minutes. Cook until mixture is heated through and fish is opaque and flaky. Thin with a little water if desired.

Servings: 4
Yield: 4

Cooking Time: 30 minutes
Total Time: 30 minutes

Nutrition Facts

Serving size: 1/4 of a recipe (7.4 ounces).

Amount Per Serving	
Calories	193.25
Calories From Fat (7%)	14.27
	% Daily Value
Total Fat 1.6g	2%
Saturated Fat 0.31g	2%
Cholesterol 86.18mg	29%
Sodium 4197mg	175%
Potassium 1145.2mg	33%
Total Carbohydrates 6.51g	2%
Fiber 2.04g	8%
Sugar 3.8g	
Protein 36.91g	74%

Shrimp Linguine

4	Tbsp	olive oil divided	1	(16 oz) package	linguine pasta, whole wheat
6		cloves garlic crushed			
3	cups	whole peeled tomatoes with liquid chopped	8	oz	small shrimp peeled and deveined
1 1/2	tsp	salt	8	oz	bay scallops
1	tsp	crushed red pepper flakes	1	Tbsp	chopped fresh parsley

Procedure

1. In a large saucepan, heat 2 tablespoons of the olive oil with the garlic over medium heat. When the garlic starts to sizzle, pour in the tomatoes. Add salt and red pepper. Bring to a boil. Lower the heat, and simmer for 30 minutes, stirring occasionally.

2. Meanwhile, bring a large pot of lightly salted water to a boil. Cook pasta according to package directions; drain.

3. In a large skillet, heat the remaining 2 tablespoons of olive oil over high heat. Add the shrimp and scallops. Cook for about 2 minutes, stirring frequently, or until the shrimp turn pink. Add shrimp and scallops to the tomato mixture, and stir in the parsley. Cook for 3 to 4 minutes, or until the sauce just begins to bubble. Serve sauce over pasta.

Servings: 8
Yield: 8

Preparation Time: 20 minutes
Cooking Time: 40 minutes
Total Time: 1 hour

Nutrition Facts

Serving size: 1/8 of a recipe (5.7 ounces).

Amount Per Serving	
Calories	109.8
Calories From Fat (58%)	63.78
	% Daily Value
Total Fat 7.22g	11%
Saturated Fat 0.99g	5%
Cholesterol 35.72mg	12%
Sodium 726.18mg	30%
Potassium 217.93mg	6%
Total Carbohydrates 6.88g	2%
Fiber 1.04g	4%
Sugar 2.17g	
Protein 5.1g	10%

Pasta

Glazed Mahi Mahi

3	Tbsp	agave nectar	2 tsp	olive oil
3	Tbsp	Bragg's liquid aminos	4 (6 oz)	mahi mahi fillets
3	Tbsp	balsamic vinegar		salt and pepper to taste
1	tsp	grated fresh ginger root	1 Tbsp	vegetable oil
1		clove garlic crushed or to taste		

Procedure

1 In a shallow glass dish, stir together the agave, Bragg's, balsamic vinegar, ginger, garlic and olive oil. Season fish fillets with salt and pepper, and place them into the dish. If the fillets have skin on them, place them skin side down. Cover, and refrigerate for 20 minutes to marinate.

2 Heat vegetable oil in a large skillet over medium-high heat. Remove fish from the dish, and reserve marinade. Fry fish for 4 to 6 minutes on each side, turning once, until fish flakes easily with a fork. Remove fillets to a serving platter and keep warm.

3 Pour reserved marinade into the skillet, and heat over medium heat until the mixture reduces to a glaze consistently. Spoon glaze over fish, and serve immediately.

Servings: 4
Yield: 4

Preparation Time: 5 minutes
Cooking Time: 12 minutes
Total Time: 37 minutes

Nutrition Facts

Serving size: 1/4 of a recipe (10.8 ounces).

Amount Per Serving	
Calories	355.43
Calories From Fat (21%)	74.82
	% Daily Value
Total Fat 8.41g	13%
Saturated Fat 1.17g	6%
Cholesterol 95.83mg	32%
Sodium 613.53mg	26%
Potassium 1299.32mg	37%
Total Carbohydrates 16.38g	5%
Fiber 0.15g	<1%
Sugar 14.95g	
Protein 50.98g	102%

Grilled Salmon

1 1/2 pound	salmon fillets	1/3 cup	Bragg's liquid aminos
	lemon pepper to taste	1/3 cup	agave nectar
	garlic powder to taste	1/3 cup	water
	salt to taste	1/4 cup	olive oil

Procedure

1 Season salmon fillets with lemon pepper, garlic powder, and salt.

2 In a small bowl, stir together Bragg's, agave, water, and oil. Place fish in a large resealable plastic bag with the sauce mixture, seal, and turn to coat. Refrigerate for at least 2 hours.

3 Preheat grill for medium heat.

4 Lightly oil grill grate. Place salmon on the preheated grill, and discard marinade. Cook salmon for 6 to 8 minutes per side, or until the fish flakes easily with a fork.

Servings: 6
Yield: 6

Preparation Time: 15 minutes
Cooking Time: 16 minutes
Total Time: 2 hours

Nutrition Facts

Serving size: 1/6 of a recipe (5.7 ounces).

Amount Per Serving	
Calories	268.58
Calories From Fat (46%)	124.6
	% Daily Value
Total Fat 14g	22%
Saturated Fat 1.73g	9%
Cholesterol 26.08mg	9%
Sodium 2792.27mg	116%
Potassium 246.47mg	7%
Total Carbohydrates 13.56g	5%
Fiber 0.16g	<1%
Sugar 12.1g	
Protein 21.56g	43%

Tuna Teriyaki

2 Tbsp Bragg's liquid aminos

1 Tbsp Chinese rice wine

1 large clove garlic minced

1 Tbsp minced fresh ginger root

4 (6 oz) tuna steaks (about 3/4 inch thick)

1 Tbsp olive oil

Procedure

1 In a shallow dish, stir together Bragg's, rice wine, garlic, and ginger. Place tuna in the marinade, and turn to coat. Cover, and refrigerate for at least 30 minutes.

2 Preheat grill for medium-high heat.

3 Remove tuna from marinade, and discard remaining liquid. Brush both sides of steaks with oil.

4 Cook tuna for approximately for 3 to 6 minutes per side, or to desired doneness.

Servings: 4
Yield: 4

Preparation Time: 15 minutes
Cooking Time: 12 minutes
Total Time: 57 minutes

Nutrition Facts

Serving size: 1/4 of a recipe (3.6 ounces).

Amount Per Serving	
Calories	163.67
Calories From Fat (42%)	68.7
	% Daily Value
Total Fat 7.68g	12%
Saturated Fat 1.33g	7%
Cholesterol 32.3mg	11%
Sodium 378.44mg	16%
Potassium 243.68mg	7%
Total Carbohydrates 1.91g	<1%
Fiber 0.05g	<1%
Sugar 1.3g	
Protein 20.44g	41%

Lemony Orange Roughy

A fast and simple recipe, yet a taste our whole family loves. Serve with a green salad.

1	Tbsp	olive oil	1	lemon, juiced
4	(4 oz)	fillets orange roughy	1/2 tsp	lemon pepper
1		orange, juiced		

Procedure

1 Heat oil in a large skillet over medium-high heat. Arrange fillets in the skillet, and drizzle with orange juice and lemon juice. Sprinkle with lemon pepper. Cook for 5 minutes, or until fish is easily flaked with a fork.

Servings: 4
Yield: 4

Preparation Time: 15 minutes
Cooking Time: 5 minutes
Total Time: 20 minutes

Nutrition Facts

Serving size: 1/4 of a recipe (4.4 ounces).

Amount Per Serving	
Calories	107.36
Calories From Fat (33%)	35.84
	% Daily Value
Total Fat 4.05g	6%
Saturated Fat 0.49g	2%
Cholesterol 51mg	17%
Sodium 61.63mg	3%
Potassium 200.21mg	6%
Total Carbohydrates 3.26g	1%
Fiber 0.09g	<1%
Sugar 2.18g	
Protein 14.15g	28%

Basil Grilled Shrimp

3	cloves	garlic minced	2	Tbsp	chopped fresh basil
1/3 cup		olive oil	1/2 tsp		salt
1/4 cup		tomato sauce	1/4 tsp		cayenne pepper
2	Tbsp	red wine vinegar	2	pounds	fresh shrimp, peeled and deveined
				Wooden skewers	

Procedure

1. In a large bowl, stir together the garlic, olive oil, tomato sauce, and red wine vinegar. Season with basil, salt, and cayenne pepper. Add shrimp to the bowl, and stir until evenly coated. Cover, and refrigerate for 30 minutes to 1 hour, stirring once or twice.
2. Preheat grill for medium heat. Thread shrimp onto skewers, piercing once near the tail and once near the head. Discard marinade.
3. Lightly oil grill grate. Cook shrimp on preheated grill for 2 to 3 minutes per side, or until opaque.

Servings: 6
Yield: 6

Preparation Time: 15 minutes
Cooking Time: 6 minutes
Total Time: 55 minutes

Nutrition Facts

Serving size: 1/6 of a recipe (6.4 ounces).

Amount Per Serving	
Calories	222.69
Calories From Fat (54%)	120.59
	% Daily Value
Total Fat 13.61g	21%
Saturated Fat 1.87g	9%
Cholesterol 190.51mg	64%
Sodium 1105.13mg	46%
Potassium 253.72mg	7%
Total Carbohydrates 3.19g	1%
Fiber 0.77g	3%
Sugar 0.48g	
Protein 21.16g	42%

Penne with Shrimp

16	oz	penne pasta, whole-wheat	1/4	cup	white wine
2	Tbsp	olive oil	2	(14.5 oz) can	diced tomatoes
1/4	cup	chopped red onion	1	pound	shrimp peeled and deveined
1	Tbsp	chopped garlic	1	cup	grated Parmesan cheese

Procedure

1 Bring a large pot of lightly salted water to a boil. Add pasta and cook for 8 to 10 minutes or until al dente; drain.

2 Heat the oil in a skillet over medium heat. Stir in onion and garlic, and cook until onion is tender. Mix in wine and tomatoes, and continue cooking 10 minutes, stirring occasionally.

3 Mix shrimp into the skillet, and cook 5 minutes, or until opaque. Toss with pasta and top with Parmesan cheese to serve.

Servings: 8
Yield: 8

Preparation Time: 10 minutes
Cooking Time: 25 minutes
Total Time: 35 minutes

Nutrition Facts

Serving size: 1/8 of a recipe (8.5 ounces).

Amount Per Serving	
Calories	353.04
Calories From Fat (20%)	69.19
	% Daily Value
Total Fat 7.67g	12%
Saturated Fat 2.71g	14%
Cholesterol 82.44mg	27%
Sodium 654.73mg	27%
Potassium 276.77mg	8%
Total Carbohydrates 47.51g	16%
Fiber 3.11g	12%
Sugar 2.56g	
Protein 20.53g	41%

Shrimp Curry

1/2 cup	rice flour	1	Tbsp	ginger garlic paste
1/2 tsp	ground turmeric	3	cups	pureed tomato
	salt to taste	1/2 tsp		kashmiri red chili powder
1	pound peeled and deveined shrimp	1/2 tsp		garam masala
3	Tbsp cooking oil	¼ tsp salt		
1	tsp cumin seeds	1/2 tsp		ground cumin
2	large onions, sliced thin	1/4 cup		coconut milk
2	green Chili peppers, halved lengthwise	1/4 cup		chopped fresh cilantro

Procedure

1. Stir the rice flour, turmeric, and salt together in a bowl; add the shrimp and turn in the flour mixture to evenly coat.

2. Heat the oil in a large skillet over medium heat; fry the cumin seeds in the hot oil until they splutter. Add the onions, green Chili peppers, and ginger-garlic paste; cook until the onions are browned, about 5 minutes. Stir the pureed tomato, Kashmiri red chili powder, garam masala, and ground cumin into the mixture. Season with salt and continue cooking until the gravy thickens and the oil is released, 10 to 15 minutes. Pour the coconut milk into the skillet and stir; lay the shrimp into the mixture and continue cooking until the shrimp are cooked through, 3 to 5 minutes more. Garnish with the cilantro to serve.

Servings: 6
Yield: 6

Preparation Time: 15 minutes
Cooking Time: 30 minutes
Total Time: 45 minutes

Nutrition Facts

Serving size: 1/6 of a recipe (9.9 ounces).

Amount Per Serving	
Calories	124.72
Calories From Fat (54%)	67.89
	% Daily Value
Total Fat 7.69g	12%
Saturated Fat 0.99g	5%
Cholesterol 0mg	0%
Sodium 240.79mg	10%
Potassium 376.76mg	11%
Total Carbohydrates 13.64g	5%
Fiber 2.46g	10%
Sugar 6.52g	
Protein 2.24g	4%

Sweet 'n' Hot Glazed Salmon

1 1/2	cup	apricot nectar	2	cloves	garlic minced
1/3	cup	chopped dried apricots	1/8	tsp	cayenne pepper
2	Tbsp	honey	1/4	tsp	ground cinnamon
2	Tbsp	Bragg's liquid aminos	1	(3/4 pound)	salmon filet without skin
1	Tbsp	grated fresh ginger			

Procedure

1. Preheat your oven's broiler, and grease a broiling pan.

2. In a saucepan over medium heat, mix together the apricot nectar, dried apricots, honey, soy sauce, ginger, garlic, cinnamon and cayenne. Bring to a boil, then reduce heat to medium-low, and simmer for about 20 minutes, or until reduced by about half. Stir occasionally to prevent burning. Remove 1/4 cup of the glaze for basting, and set the remaining aside.

3. Place the salmon filet on the greased broiling pan, and brush with glaze. Broil 3 inches from the heat for 8 to 12 minutes or until salmon flakes easily with a fork. Gently turn over once during cooking, and baste frequently during the last 4 minutes. Serve with remaining glaze.

Servings: 4
Yield: 4

Preparation Time: 30 minutes
Cooking Time: 12 minutes
Total Time: 42 minutes

Nutrition Facts

Serving size: 1/4 of a recipe (5.3 ounces).

Amount Per Serving	
Calories	200.98
Calories From Fat (13%)	27.11
	% Daily Value
Total Fat 3.03g	5%
Saturated Fat 0.66g	3%
Cholesterol 38.75mg	13%
Sodium 17.56mg	<1%
Potassium 492.59mg	14%
Total Carbohydrates 29.9g	10%
Fiber 1.54g	6%
Sugar 27.44g	
Protein 16.04g	32%

Szechwan Shrimp

4	Tbsp	water	1/4 tsp		ground ginger
2	Tbsp	ketchup	1	Tbsp	vegetable oil
1	Tbsp	Bragg's liquid aminos	1/4 cup		sliced green onion
2	tsp	cornstarch	4	cloves	garlic minced
1	tsp	agave nectar	12	ounces	cooked shrimp tail removed
1/2 tsp		crushed red pepper			

Procedure

1. In a bowl, stir together water, ketchup, Bragg's, cornstarch, agave, crushed red pepper, and ground ginger. Set aside.
2. Heat oil in a large skillet over medium-high heat. Stir in green onions and garlic; cook 30 seconds. Stir in shrimp, and toss to coat with oil. Stir in sauce. Cook and stir until sauce is bubbly and thickened.

Servings: 4
Yield: 4

Preparation Time: 10 minutes
Cooking Time: 10 minutes
Total Time: 20 minutes

Nutrition Facts

Serving size: 1/4 of a recipe (4.5 ounces).

Amount Per Serving	
Calories	158.45
Calories From Fat (28%)	44.45
	% Daily Value
Total Fat 5g	8%
Saturated Fat 0.43g	2%
Cholesterol 179.35mg	60%
Sodium 1023.98mg	43%
Potassium 211.25mg	6%
Total Carbohydrates 7.65g	3%
Fiber 0.3g	1%
Sugar 3.39g	
Protein 20.02g	40%

Tomato Fish Stew

3 1/2 oz	Sun Dried Tomatoes	4	Tbsp	thyme
		2		bay leaves
2 Tbsp	olive oil	1/2 cup		kalamata olives
1 large	yellow onion chopped			sliced
1	green bell pepper chopped	1	(15 oz) can	navy beans, drained and rinsed
2 (8 oz) bottles	clam juice	1	pound	grouper, cut into 1 inch pieces
2 (14 oz) can	diced tomatoes (no salt added)	2	tsp	fennel seeds, lightly crushed
1 cup	dry red wine (or substitute broth or tomato juice)	1	pinch	salt and pepper to taste
4 cloves	garlic crushed	1/2 cup		grated Parmesan cheese

Procedure

1 In a pan, simmer sun-dried tomatoes in 1 1/2 cups water until very soft; discard water.

2 Sauté onion and green pepper in oil over medium heat until softened.

3 In a food processor or blender, combine sun-dried tomatoes and 1 bottle clam juice until smooth; add to pot. Stir in remaining clam juice, diced tomatoes, wine, garlic, Thyme, bay leaves and olives. Simmer 20 minutes.

4 Add beans, fish, fennel seeds, salt and pepper. Simmer until fish is done, about 10 minutes. Remove bay leaves. Ladle into bowls; sprinkle with cheese.

Servings: 8
Yield: 8

Nutrition Facts

Serving size: 1/8 of a recipe (7.2 ounces).

Amount Per Serving	
Calories	268.33
Calories From Fat (25%)	66.23
	% Daily Value
Total Fat 7.55g	12%
Saturated Fat 1.73g	9%
Cholesterol 10.38mg	3%
Sodium 629.77mg	26%
Potassium 1272.43mg	36%
Total Carbohydrates 33.27g	11%
Fiber 10.03g	40%
Sugar 10.99g	
Protein 15.03g	30%

Vegetable

Asian Tofu Steaks

2	(1 pound) blocks	extra firm tofu	1	Tbsp	fresh ginger, grated
1	cup	vegetable broth	1	tsp	orange zest
			1/2 tsp	cornstarch
3	Tbsp	Bragg's liquid aminos		Vegetable oil cooking spray
1	Tbsp	hoisin sauce		20 wooden skewers, soaked for 1 hr in warm water
1	Tbsp	dry sherry		
1	Tbsp	agave nectar	1/4 cup	scallions, sliced for garnish
2	cloves	garlic, minced		

Procedure

1. Wrap blocks of tofu in 2 layers of paper towels. Place tofu on a plate. Place another plate on top and then place a weight on the top plate (a heavy pan will do). Press for about 1 to 2 hours in the refrigerator.

2. Remove paper towels from tofu and drain all excess water. Pat the tofu dry. Slice the tofu into 3/4 inch slices.

3. In a medium bowl, whisk together broth, Bragg's, hoisin sauce, sherry, agave nectar, garlic, ginger and orange zest. Arrange tofu in a shallow baking dish. Pour marinade over tofu and marinate, covered, in the refrigerator for 2 hrs. Turn tofu slices after one hour.

4. Remove tofu from baking dish and set on a large cutting board. Place marinade in a saucepan and bring to a boil. In a small bowl, combine cornstarch with 2 tsp water and mix well. Add to marinade and cooked until thickened, about 1 min. Set aside. Coat an outdoor grill well with cooking spray and set the temp to high heat.

5. Skewer the tofu.

6. Place the tofu on the grill and cook on one side for about 4 min. basting with some of the reserved marinade. Turn and grill tofu for another 4 min., continuing to baste with reserved marinade. Remove tofu to a platter and drizzle with any remaining sauce. Sprinkle with scallions

Servings: 5
Yield: 5

Preparation Time: 4 hours
Cooking Time: 15 minutes

Nutrition Facts

Serving size:
1/5 of a
recipe (3.8
ounces).

Amount Per Serving	
Calories	51.74
Calories From Fat (16%)	8.17
	% Daily Value
Total Fat 0.9g	1%
Saturated Fat 0.14g	<1%
Cholesterol 0.1mg	<1%
Sodium 184.35mg	8%
Potassium 84.83mg	2%
Total Carbohydrates 7.69g	3%
Fiber 0.36g	1%
Sugar 5.2g	
Protein 2.81g	6%

Butter Chickpea Curry

If you like Indian food, this chickpea curry tastes as authentic as they get. Make sure to allow plenty of time for the spices to blend. It tastes even better the next day!

4	medium	potatoes cubed	2	tsp	cumin
2	Tbsp	canola oil	1	tsp	salt
1	medium	yellow onion diced	1/2	cup	peas
2	tsp	minced garlic	1	can (15 oz)	diced tomatoes with green chili peppers
4	tsp	curry powder			
4	tsp	garam masala	1	(12 oz) can	chickpeas rinsed and drained
2	tsp	ground ginger			
1/4	tsp	red pepper flakes	1	Tablespoon	tomato paste
			1/2	cup	coconut milk

Procedure

1. Place potatoes in a saucepan, cover with water, and bring to a boil over high heat; simmer until the potatoes are tender. Drain, and set aside.

2. Warm oil in a large saucepan over medium heat. Stir in onion and garlic, and cook until the onions are soft and translucent. Stir in curry powder, garam masala, ginger, cumin, red pepper flakes and salt. Cook for 1 or 2 minutes, stirring. Pour in tomatoes, peas, tomato paste and chickpeas. Stir in potatoes. Cover pan. Simmer 30 minutes with stove on low setting. Let sit on the stove with heat off for 30 minutes to allow spices to blend.

Servings: 4
Yield: 4

Preparation Time: 10 minutes
Cooking Time: 40 minutes
Total Time: 50 minutes

Nutrition Facts

Serving size: 1/4 of a recipe (14.9 ounces).

Amount Per Serving	
Calories	383.11
Calories From Fat (20%)	77.16
	% Daily Value
Total Fat 8.82g	14%
Saturated Fat 0.78g	4%
Cholesterol 0.62mg	<1%
Sodium 1034.79mg	43%
Potassium 1293.71mg	37%
Total Carbohydrates 67.1g	22%
Fiber 9.89g	40%
Sugar 6.77g	
Protein 11.03g	22%

Curry Tofu

2	bunches	green onions	1	pound	firm tofu cut into 3/4 inch cubes
1	(14 oz) can	light coconut milk	4		roma (plum) tomatoes, chopped
1/4	cup	Bragg's liquid aminos, divided	1		yellow bell pepper, thinly sliced
1/2	tsp	agave nectar	4	oz	fresh mushrooms, chopped
1 1/2	tsp	curry powder			
1	tsp	minced fresh ginger	1/4	cup	chopped fresh basil
			4	cups	chopped bok choy
2	tsp	chili paste			salt to taste

Procedure

1. Finely chop green onions.
2. In a large heavy skillet over medium heat, mix coconut milk, 3 tablespoons Bragg's, agave, curry powder, ginger, and chili paste. Bring to a boil.
3. Stir tofu, tomatoes, yellow pepper, mushrooms, and finely chopped green onions into the skillet. Cover, and cook 5 minutes, stirring occasionally. Mix in basil and bok choy. Season with salt and remaining Bragg's. Continue cooking 5 minutes, or until vegetables are tender but crisp.

Servings: 6
Yield: 6

Preparation Time: 25 minutes
Cooking Time: 15 minutes
Total Time: 40 minutes

Nutrition Facts

Serving size: 1/6 of a recipe (11.4 ounces).

Amount Per Serving	
Calories	128.4
Calories From Fat (33%)	42.27
	% Daily Value
Total Fat 5.06g	**8%**
Saturated Fat 0.55g	**3%**
Cholesterol 0mg	**0%**
Sodium 452.92mg	**19%**
Potassium 741.94mg	**21%**
Total Carbohydrates 13.69g	**5%**
Fiber 4.51g	**18%**
Sugar 5.07g	
Protein 11.71g	**23%**

Grilled Portobello Mushroom

6	medium	Portobello mushrooms	1 Tbsp	garlic minced
6	cloves	garlic minced	½ tsp	salt
6	Tbsp	lemon juice	½ tsp	black pepper
6	Tbsp	balsamic vinegar		Vegetable oil cooking spray
3	Tbsp	chopped fresh basil		

Procedure

1. Remove stems from mushrooms and discard. Rinse mushroom caps to remove any surface dirt.

2. Tuck garlic into the gills of the mushrooms. Space out so the entire mushroom has garlic divided throughout.

3. Place mushrooms in a large baking pan. Mix together the lemon juice, vinegar, basil, minced garlic, salt and black pepper. Pour over the mushrooms and let marinate for 1-2 hrs.

4. Remove the mushrooms from the marinade. Coat a grill rack with cooking spray. Grill the mushrooms over medium-high heat, turning once, about 2 to 3 min per side, basting with any leftover marinade.

Servings: 6

Preparation Time: 2 hours
Cooking Time: 10 minutes

Nutrition Facts

Serving size: 1/6 of a recipe (4.4 ounces).

Amount Per Serving	
Calories	50.08
Calories From Fat (10%)	4.84
	% Daily Value
Total Fat 0.57g	<1%
Saturated Fat 0.13g	<1%
Cholesterol 0mg	0%
Sodium 61.12mg	3%
Potassium 426.66mg	12%
Total Carbohydrates 9.84g	3%
Fiber 2.15g	9%
Sugar 5.01g	
Protein 2.78g	6%

Potato and Cheddar Soup

2	cups	water		salt and pepper to taste
2	cups	peeled and cubed red potatoes	3 cups	milk
			1/2 tsp	agave nectar
3	Tbsp	melted butter	1 cup	shredded Cheddar cheese
1	small	onion chopped		
3	Tbsp	all purpose flour	1 cup	diced ham

Procedure

5 Using a medium sized stock pot bring water to a boil, add potatoes and cook until tender. Drain reserving 1 cup liquid.

6 Stir in butter, onion and flour. Season with salt and pepper. Gradually stir in potatoes, reserved liquid, milk, agave, cheese, and ham. Simmer for 30 minutes, stirring frequently.

Servings: 10
Yield: 10

Nutrition Facts

Serving size: 1/10 of a recipe (7.1 ounces).

Amount Per Serving	
Calories	168.34
Calories From Fat (48%)	81.34
	% Daily Value
Total Fat 9.23g	14%
Saturated Fat 5.66g	28%
Cholesterol 30.98mg	10%
Sodium 196.91mg	8%
Potassium 275.96mg	8%
Total Carbohydrates 14.32g	5%
Fiber 0.87g	3%
Sugar 4.68g	
Protein 7.51g	15%

Vegetable Koora

2	Tbsp	olive oil	1/2	tsp	ground turmeric
2		dried red chili peppers, broken into pieces	4		medium tomatoes chopped
1	tsp	cumin seeds	1/2	tsp	red chili powder
1	tsp	mustard seed	1	tsp	agave nectar
1/4	tsp	asafoetida powder			salt to taste
1		spring fresh curry leaves	1/2	cup	water
2		onions, chopped	2	Tbsp	chopped cilantro leaves for garnish (optional)
2		green chili peppers, chopped			

Procedure

1 Heat the oil in a large skillet over medium heat; fry the red chili peppers, cumin seeds, and mustard seeds in the hot oil until the seeds begin to splutter, 2 to 3 minutes. Sprinkle the asafoetida powder over the seeds and add the curry leaves. Stir the onions, green chili peppers, and turmeric powder into the mixture; cook and stir until the onions are softened, 3 to 5 minutes. Add the tomatoes, red chili powder, and salt; continue cooking until the tomatoes are pulpy. Pour the water into the mixture; simmer until the curry begins to thicken, 5 to 10 minutes. Garnish with cilantro to serve.

Servings: 4
Yield: 4

Preparation Time: 10 minutes
Cooking Time: 15 minutes
Total Time: 25 minutes

Nutrition Facts

Serving size: 1/4 of a recipe (10.8 ounces).

Amount Per Serving	
Calories	133.64
Calories From Fat (49%)	64.93
	% Daily Value
Total Fat 7.37g	11%
Saturated Fat 1.03g	5%
Cholesterol 0mg	0%
Sodium 87.93mg	4%
Potassium 579.25mg	17%
Total Carbohydrates 16.57g	6%
Fiber 3.47g	14%
Sugar 9.55g	
Protein 2.86g	6%

Vegetarian Chili

1	Tbsp	olive oil	2	(4 ounce) can	chopped green chili peppers, drained
1/2		medium onion chopped			
2		bay leaves	2	(12 oz) package	vegetarian burger crumbles
1	tsp	ground cumin			
2	Tbsp	dried oregano	3	(28 oz) can	whole peeled tomatoes crushed
1	Tbsp	salt			
2	stalks	celery chopped	1/4	cup	chili powder
2		green bell pepper chopped	1	Tbsp	ground black pepper
2		jalapeno pepper chopped	1	(15 oz) can	kidney beans drained
3	cloves	garlic chopped	1	(15 oz) can	garbanzo beans, drained
			1	(15 oz) can	black beans
			1	(15 oz) can	whole kernel corn

Procedure

1 Heat the olive oil in a large pot over medium heat. Stir in the onion, and season with bay leaves, cumin, oregano, and salt. Cook and stir until onion is tender, then mix in the celery, green bell peppers, jalapeno peppers, garlic, and green chili peppers. When vegetables are heated through, mix in the vegetarian burger crumbles. Reduce heat to low, cover pot, and simmer 5 minutes.

2 Mix the tomatoes into the pot. Season chili with chili powder and pepper. Stir in the kidney beans, garbanzo beans, and black beans. Bring to a boil, reduce heat to low, and simmer 45 minutes. Stir in the corn, and continue cooking 5 minutes before serving.

Servings: 8
Yield: 8

Preparation Time: 15 minutes
Cooking Time: 1 hour
Total Time: 1 hour and 15 minutes

Nutrition Facts

Serving size: 1/8 of a recipe (19.1 ounces).

Amount Per Serving	
Calories	232.41
Calories From Fat (14%)	31.82
	% Daily Value
Total Fat 3.71g	6%
Saturated Fat 0.58g	3%
Cholesterol 0mg	0%
Sodium 1778.29mg	74%
Potassium 1130.45mg	32%
Total Carbohydrates 44.55g	15%
Fiber 13.32g	53%
Sugar 10.75g	
Protein 10.92g	22%

Vegetarian Chili II

1	bag	Morningstar Farm veggie crumble	1 1/2	tsp	garlic powder
46	oz	tomato juice	1	tsp	salt
1	can (15 oz)	tomato sauce	1/2	tsp	black pepper
1 1/2	cup	chopped onion	1/2	tsp	dried oregano
1/2	cup	chopped celery	1/2	tsp	xylitol
1/4	cup	chopped green bell pepper	1/8	tsp	cayenne pepper, ground
1/4	cup	chili powder	2	cups	canned beans
2	tsp	cumin			

Procedure

Combine ingredients and cook for at least 1.5 hours in a saucepan or 4 hours in a slow cooker on "high".

Servings: 8
Yield: 8

Nutrition Facts

Serving size: 1/8 of a recipe (12.2 ounces).

Amount Per Serving	
Calories	173.96
Calories From Fat (12%)	20.88
	% Daily Value
Total Fat 2.4g	4%
Saturated Fat 0.35g	2%
Cholesterol 0mg	0%
Sodium 968.7mg	40%
Potassium 938.84mg	27%
Total Carbohydrates 29.34g	10%
Fiber 8.71g	35%
Sugar 10.7g	
Protein 12.54g	25%

Baked Eggplant Salad

1	pound	eggplant	2	tsp	red wine vinegar
2		red bell pepper	2	tsp	Dijon mustard
2		tomatoes seeded and chopped	1/2 tsp		agave nectar
2	cloves	garlic, minced			kosher or sea salt to taste
1/4 cup		finely chopped red onion			Freshly ground black pepper to taste
1/4 cup		fresh parsley, finely chopped			

Procedure

1. Preheat the oven to 400°F. Remove the stem from the eggplant and cut the eggplant in half and remove the seeds and membrane. Place the eggplant and peppers on a baking sheet covered with parchment paper and roast for about 25 to 30 min until soft. Place the peppers in a bowl and cover with plastic wrap, until cool enough to handle.
2. Peel the skin off the peppers and cut into strips. Scoop out the flesh of the eggplant and mash, and then drain any extra liquid.
3. Place the peppers and eggplant in a large bowl. Add the tomatoes, garlic, onion and parsley. In a small bowl, mix together the vinegar, mustard, agave, salt and black pepper. Pour the dressing onto the salad and mix well. Cover and refrigerate for at least 1 hour prior to serving.

Servings: 6

Preparation Time: 10 minutes plus 1hr resting time
Cooking Time: 50 minutes

Nutrition Facts

Serving size: 1/6 of a recipe (5.9 ounces).

Amount Per Serving	
Calories	45.48
Calories From Fat (9%)	4.01
	% Daily Value
Total Fat 0.48g	<1%
Saturated Fat 0.05g	<1%
Cholesterol 0mg	0%
Sodium 75.55mg	3%
Potassium 355.9mg	10%
Total Carbohydrates 9.7g	3%
Fiber 4.15g	17%
Sugar 3.93g	
Protein 1.75g	4%

Black Beans and Rice

A Mexican staple, the combination of black beans and rice provides a complete protein. Top with chopped lettuce, tomato, salsa, and avocado for a filling dish.

1 2/3	cup	vegetable broth	2	Tbsp	fresh cilantro, finely chopped
1/4	cup	shallot finely chopped	2	Tbsp	finely chopped scallions
2	tsp	garlic, minced	1	(15 oz) can	black beans, drained and rinsed
2/3	cup	brown rice, rinsed	½	tsp	kosher or sea salt to taste
1/4	tsp	ground cumin	½	tsp	Ground black pepper to taste

Chopped lettuce, tomato, and avocado as garnish

Salsa to taste

Procedure

1 Heat 1/3 cup broth in a large saucepan over medium heat. Add shallots and garlic and sauté for 3 min. Add rice and cumin and sauté for 2 min.

2 Add remaining 11/3 cup broth and bring to a boil. Cover and simmer on low heat for about 45 min., or until rice is tender. Add cilantro, scallions, beans, salt and black pepper and mix well.

Servings: 4
Yield: 4

Preparation Time: 10 minutes
Cooking Time: 50 minutes

Nutrition Facts

Serving size: 1/4 of a recipe (11.6 ounces).

Amount Per Serving	
Calories	193.37
Calories From Fat (6%)	10.72
	% Daily Value
Total Fat 1.3g	2%
Saturated Fat 0.07g	<1%
Cholesterol 0mg	0%
Sodium 725.05mg	30%
Potassium 209.37mg	6%
Total Carbohydrates 42.48g	14%
Fiber 5.94g	24%
Sugar 2.09g	
Protein 6.27g	13%

Chilied Great Northern Beans

2	(15 oz) can	great northern beans, drained and rinsed	1	Tbsp	agave nectar light
1	medium	onion chopped	1	tsp	chili powder
2	cloves	garlic, minced	1/2	tsp	dry mustard
3	Tbsp	canned, chopped green chilies or 1 small fresh jalapeño			kosher or sea salt to taste
1	(10 oz) can	diced tomatoes, with liquid			Freshly ground black pepper to taste
2	Tbsp	apple cider vinegar			

Procedure

1. Preheat the oven to 350°F. Combine all ingredients in a 1-quart casserole dish. Cover and bake for 30 min.
2. Uncover and bake for an additional 20 to 30 min.

Servings: 4
Yield: 4

Preparation Time: 10 minutes
Cooking Time: 30 minutes

Nutrition Facts

Serving size: 1/4 of a recipe (13.4 ounces).

Amount Per Serving	
Calories	218.46
Calories From Fat (4%)	8.18
	% Daily Value
Total Fat 0.98g	2%
Saturated Fat 0.23g	1%
Cholesterol 0mg	0%
Sodium 398.44mg	17%
Potassium 912.17mg	26%
Total Carbohydrates 43.74g	15%
Fiber 9.32g	37%
Sugar 10.3g	
Protein 11.83g	24%

Curried Quorn Kabobs

For the Marinade:

1 tsp	3/4 cup canned lite coconut milk
1 (8 oz) can	tomato sauce
1	garlic clove, minced
3 Tbsp	curry powder
1 tsp	ground black pepper
1 tsp	ground cumin
1 tsp	onion powder

For the Kabobs:

1	package Quorn chunks
1	onion cut into wedges
12	cherry or grape tomatoes
12	mushrooms
1	bell pepper, seeded and cut into wedges

Procedure

1. In a small bowl, mix together all marinade ingredients.
2. Begin to assemble kabobs by placing vegetables and Quorn on skewers.
3. Soak kabobs in marinade for a minimum of 15 min., up to 1 day in the refrigerator.
4. When ready to cook kabobs, preheat the broiler or grill to medium high.
5. Cook for 10 min, turning and brushing with marinade as needed. Cook for 10 additional minutes and remove from heat. Serve immediately.

Servings: 4
Yield: 4

Preparation Time: 20 minutes plus 15 minutes resting time
Cooking Time: 20 minutes

Nutrition Facts

Serving size: 1/4 of a recipe (17.4 ounces).

Amount Per Serving	
Calories	185.88
Calories From Fat (26%)	47.79
	% Daily Value
Total Fat 5.75g	9%
Saturated Fat 1g	5%
Cholesterol 0mg	0%
Sodium 352.66mg	15%
Potassium 1214.13mg	35%
Total Carbohydrates 26.03g	9%
Fiber 5.52g	22%
Sugar 6.58g	
Protein 13.09g	26%

Curried Vegetables

1/4	cup	vegetable broth	1/4	tsp	turmeric
1	large	onion chopped	1/4	cup	chopped fresh cilantro
4	clove	garlic, minced	1	Tbsp	Bragg's liquid aminos
2	Tbsp	fresh ginger, minced	2	small	sweet potatoes, peeled and cut into 1/4-inch cubes
1		jalapeño pepper, chopped			
2/3	cup	tomato puree	1/2	head	cauliflower, separated into florets
1	tsp	ground coriander			
1	tsp	ground cumin	2	cups	frozen green peas, thawed

Procedure

1. Heat broth in a large skillet over medium heat. Put in the onion, garlic, ginger and hot pepper. Sauté for 5 to 6 min. Stir in 3 tbsp water and cook for 3 min.

2. Stir in tomato puree, coriander, cumin, turmeric, cilantro, Bragg's, and sweet potatoes. Cover skillet. Cook for 15 min.

3. Add the cauliflower, cover and simmer for 15 to 20 min. Add peas and cook for 5 additional min.

Servings: 4
Yield: 4

Preparation Time: 20 minutes
Cooking Time: 45 minutes

Nutrition Facts

Serving size: 1/4 of a recipe (9.3 ounces).

Amount Per Serving	
Calories	140.65
Calories From Fat (4%)	5.74
	% Daily Value
Total Fat 0.69g	1%
Saturated Fat 0.11g	<1%
Cholesterol 0mg	0%
Sodium 314.05mg	13%
Potassium 657.08mg	19%
Total Carbohydrates 30.42g	10%
Fiber 6.89g	28%
Sugar 9.42g	
Protein 5.58g	11%

Moroccan Stew

I make this soup in a Crockpot. Simply place all ingredients in the pot and cook on low for 6-8 hours. If you want to follow the directions to make the soup on a stove, you should add 1T butter to the ingredients list. If you prefer a creamy soup, add a tablespoon of warm, heavy cream for each serving.

1/2		cinnamon stick	1	14.5 oz	diced tomatoes, undrained
1	tsp	ground cumin			
1/2	tsp	ground ginger	1	Tbsp	agave nectar
1/4	tsp	ground cloves	2		large carrots, chopped
1/4	tsp	ground nutmeg			
1/4	tsp	ground turmeric	1		sweet potatoes, peeled and diced
2	tsp	curry powder			
1	tsp	salt	2		large potatoes, peeled and diced
1	tsp	butter			
1/2		sweet onion chopped	1 can	15 oz	garbanzo beans, drained
1	cup	finely shredded kale	1/4	cup	chopped dried apricots
2 cans	14 oz	organic vegetable broth	1/2	cup	dried lentils, rinsed
			1/2	tsp	Ground black pepper, to taste
			1	Tbsp	cornstarch (optional)
			1	Tbsp	water (optional)

Procedure

1 Combine cinnamon, cumin, ginger, cloves, nutmeg, turmeric, curry powder, and salt in a large bowl, reserve.

2 Melt butter in a large pot over medium heat. Cook the onion in the butter until soft and just beginning to brown, 5 to 10 minutes. Stir in the shredded kale and reserved spice mixture. Cook for 2 minutes or until kale begins to wilt and spices are fragrant.

3 Pour the vegetable broth into the pot. Stir in the tomatoes, agave, carrots, sweet potatoes, potatoes, garbanzo beans, dried apricots, salt, pepper and lentils. Bring to boil; reduce heat to low.

4 Simmer stew for 30 minutes or until the vegetables and lentils are cooked and tender. Season with black pepper to taste. If desired, combine optional cornstarch and water; stir into stew. Simmer until stew has thickened, about 5 minutes.

Servings: 6
Yield: 6

Preparation Time: 30 minutes
Cooking Time: 40 minutes
Total Time: 1 hour and 10 minutes

Nutrition Facts

Serving size: 1/6 of a recipe (10.6 ounces).

Amount Per Serving	
Calories	543
Calories From Fat (7%)	36.77
	% Daily Value
Total Fat 4.2g	6%
Saturated Fat 1.5g	8%
Cholesterol 5mg	2%
Sodium 1218mg	51%
Potassium 2046mg	58%
Total Carbohydrates 110.6g	37%
Fiber 24g	96%
Sugar 23.2g	
Protein 19.5g	39%

Roasted Pepper and Zucchini Fettuccini

1	large	red bell pepper	1/2	cup	dry white wine
1	large	yellow bell pepper			
1/4	cup	vegetable broth	1	Tbsp	lemon juice
1	large	onion, halved and sliced	2	tsp	fresh thyme
			1	(10 oz) package	Fettuccine pasta, whole wheat
3		garlic clove minced			
2	medium	zucchini, sliced into 1/4 inch thick rounds	1	pinch	sea salt
					Freshly ground black pepper to taste
	pinch	crushed red pepper			
			1/4	cup	Parmesan cheese

Procedure

1. Cut the peppers in half and remove the seeds and white membrane. Place the pepper halves on a broiler pan. Broil the peppers skin-side up until the skin blackens. Place the pepper halves in a bowl, cover with plastic wrap and allow to cool.

2. When the peppers have cooled enough to handle, removed the blackened skin with your fingertips and cut each pepper into 4 pieces. Discard the seeds and white membrane if you haven't done so already. Cut the peppers into 1-inch strips and set aside.

3. Heat the vegetable broth in a large skillet over medium heat. Put in the garlic and onion and sauté for 5 to 6 min. Add the zucchini and crushed red pepper and sauté for about 15 min. Add the roasted peppers, wine, lemon juice and thyme. Sauté for 1 min.

4. Cook the fettuccine according to package directions. Drain the pasta, immediately toss with the vegetable mixture, sprinkle with Parmesan cheese and then serve.

Servings: 4
Yield: 4

Preparation Time: 15 minutes
Cooking Time: 50 minutes

Nutrition Facts

Serving size: 1/4 of a recipe (10.2 ounces).

Amount Per Serving	
Calories	191.99
Calories From Fat (12%)	22.97
	% Daily Value
Total Fat 2.61g	4%
Saturated Fat 1.11g	6%
Cholesterol 3.75mg	1%
Sodium 272.01mg	11%
Potassium 594.48mg	17%
Total Carbohydrates 33.83g	11%
Fiber 3.86g	15%
Sugar 6.07g	
Protein 8.14g	16%

Spicy Spaghetti

My meat-eating husband can't tell the difference between ground beef and tofu crumbles. You'll find them in the refrigerated section of the grocery store, near other tofu and vegetarian items.

1 package	Marjon vegetarian hamburger tofu crumbles	1 Tbsp	fresh oregano
		1 Tbsp	fresh thyme
2	jalapenos	1 16 oz package	corn spaghetti
1 can (15 oz)	crushed tomatoes	¼ cup cheese	Parmesan
1 jar	spaghetti sauce		

Procedure

1. Combine all ingredients except for spaghetti in a large saucepan.
2. Bring to a boil and then reduce heat to simmer.
3. Cover pan and simmer for 1 hour.
4. Remove jalapenos with 1 cup sauce and blend until jalapenos are well mixed.
5. Return jalapeno mix to pan and stir well.
6. Cook spaghetti according to package directions. Serve spaghetti with sauce on top and Parmesan.

Servings: 4
Yield: 4

Nutrition Facts

Serving size: 1/4 of a recipe (10.9 ounces).

Amount Per Serving	
Calories	165.54
Calories From Fat (19%)	31.24
	% Daily Value
Total Fat 3.6g	6%
Saturated Fat 0.67g	3%
Cholesterol 1.29mg	<1%
Sodium 550.71mg	23%
Potassium 671.97mg	19%
Total Carbohydrates 29.3g	10%
Fiber 4.5g	18%
Sugar 10.85g	
Protein 7.22g	14%

Recipe Tips

If you can't find tofu crumbles, try Quorn crumbles or any vegetarian ground beef substitute.

Author Notes

Think tofu is tasteless? Think again! This recipe is loved by our entire family, who swear it must be ground beef.

Lentil and Rice Stuffed Cabbage

1		onion, chopped	1/4 cup	tomato paste
1/4 cup		vegetable broth	1/2 cup	crushed walnuts
4	cloves	garlic, minced	1/2 cup	dried brown lentils
1/2 tsp		cumin seeds	1/2 cup	long grain brown rice
1/2 tsp		black pepper	3/4 tsp	salt
1	tsp	coriander seeds	1	small head green cabbage

Procedure

1. Over medium heat, Sauté onion in a saucepan with broth until onion browns. Add garlic, cumin, black pepper and coriander and sauté for 2 min. Add the tomato paste and sauté for another 3 min., stirring the whole time. Stir in 2 cups water until well mixed and bring to a boil.

2. Add the walnuts, lentils and rice. Cover pan, then allow water to boil again and then reduce heat to low. Cook for 20 min.

3. While lentils and rice are cooking, tear the leaves off the cabbage and steam them until they are soft, about 20 min.

4. Stuff cabbage leaves with lentil and rice mixture, rolling the leaves closed and then folding the sides over.

Servings: 8
Yield: 8

Preparation Time: 5 minutes
Cooking Time: 45 minutes

Nutrition Facts

Serving size: 1/8 of a recipe (2.7 ounces).

Amount Per Serving	
Calories	152.67
Calories From Fat (30%)	45.08
	% Daily Value
Total Fat 5.38g	8%
Saturated Fat 0.56g	3%
Cholesterol 0mg	0%
Sodium 304.75mg	13%
Potassium 309.88mg	9%
Total Carbohydrates 21.62g	7%
Fiber 5.6g	22%
Sugar 2.62g	
Protein 5.95g	12%

Traffic Light Peppers

1	cup	brown basmati rice	1	tsp	dried oregano
2	medium	red bell pepper	1/4	tsp	sea salt
2	medium	yellow bell peppers	1/4	tsp	ground black pepper
2	medium	green bell peppers			
1/4	cup	vegetable broth	1	(15 oz) can	black beans, drained and rinsed
1	cup	chopped onion			
1	tsp	chili powder	1 cup	brown rice, cooked	
1	tsp	ground cumin			
			1	cup	seeded and chopped tomato
			8	slices	Cheddar cheese

Procedure

1. Cook rice according to package directions.
2. Preheat the oven to 400°F.
3. Cut each bell pepper in half lengthwise. Remove seeds and ribs. Bring a large saucepan of water to a boil. Add the bell pepper halves and blanch for about 4 min. Drain and pat dry.
4. Heat the oil in a skillet over medium heat. Add the onion and sauté for about 3 min. Add chili powder, cumin, oregano, salt and black pepper. Sauté for 1 min. Add the beans, rice and tomato and sauté for 2 min.
5. Stuffed bell peppers with the mixture, packing them well. Top each bell pepper with a slice of cheese. Place in an 8x8-inch baking dish.
6. Bake bell peppers, uncovered for about 20 min. Set oven to a broil. Broil bell peppers for 1 to 2 min., until the top is browned and cheese is bubbly.

Servings: 4
Yield: 4

Preparation Time: 15 minutes
Cooking Time: 30 minutes

Nutrition Facts

Serving size: 1/4 of a recipe (17 ounces).

Amount Per Serving	
Calories	562.63
Calories From Fat (34%)	190.41
	% Daily Value
Total Fat 21.74g	33%
Saturated Fat 12.19g	61%
Cholesterol 59.65mg	20%
Sodium 2028.49mg	85%
Potassium 880.78mg	25%
Total Carbohydrates 73.26g	24%
Fiber 12.13g	49%
Sugar 8.49g	
Protein 24.63g	49%

Stuffed Portobello Mushrooms with Brown Rice

1	cup	short-grain brown rice	3	Tbsp finely chopped fresh parsley
1/4 cup	finely chopped onion			
1/2 cup	finely chopped carrot	1	Tbsp	chopped fresh chives
1	tsp	dried basil	1/2 tsp	salt
1/2 tsp	dried oregano	½ tsp	black pepper
1/2 cup	chopped red tomato	4	Portobello mushrooms cap
1/2 cup	chopped yellow tomato		Vegetable oil cooking spray
			1/4 cup	parmesan cheese

Procedure

1 Cook rice according to package directions. During the last 5 min. of cooking time, add onion, carrot, basil and oregano.

2 In a bowl, combine cooked rice, tomatoes, parsley, chives, salt and black pepper. Set aside. Preheat the oven broiler.

3 Remove the gills from the undersides of the mushrooms using a spoon; discard gills. Place the mushrooms, gill side down, on a foil lined broiler tray that has been coated with cooking spray. Broil mushrooms for about 5 min.

4 Turn mushrooms over and stuff each mushroom with equal amounts of the rice mixture. Sprinkle each with parmesan. Broil mushrooms for about 5 to 6 min. until lightly browned.

Servings: 4
Yield: 4

Preparation Time: 20 minutes
Cooking Time: 1 hour

Nutrition Facts

Serving size: 1/4 of a recipe (9.4 ounces).

Amount Per Serving	
Calories	222.72
Calories From Fat (13%)	27.93
	% Daily Value
Total Fat 3.28g	5%
Saturated Fat 0.94g	5%
Cholesterol 3.6mg	1%
Sodium 489.96mg	20%
Potassium 255.74mg	7%
Total Carbohydrates 46.88g	16%
Fiber 4.54g	18%
Sugar 3.25g	
Protein 6.33g	13%

Sweet and Sour Tofu

For the Sauce:		
1/3 cup	pineapple juice
2	Tbsp	red wine vinegar
2	Tbsp	agave nectar
1	tsp	Bragg's liquid aminos
1	tsp	fresh ginger, grated
2	cloves	garlic, minced
2	tsp	arrowroot

For the tofu:		
1/2 cup		Pamela's Gluten-free baking mix
1	(1 pound)	package extra-firm tofu, cut into cubes
2	tbsp	olive oil
1		red bell pepper, thinly sliced
1		green bell pepper, thinly sliced
1/2	large	red onion, thinly sliced
1/2	cup	drained, canned pineapple chunks packed in juice

Procedure

1. Combine all sauce ingredients in a measuring cup and set aside.
2. Pour the baking mix into pie pan, and lightly dredge tofu in the mix. Shake off excess mix.
3. Heat the oil in a large skillet over medium heat. Sauté tofu until golden brown on both sides, about 7 to 8 min.
4. Remove tofu from skillet. Add the bell peppers and onions and stir-fry for 5 min. Add the pineapple and sauce and cook until sauce thickens, about 1 min.

Servings: 4
Yield: 4

Preparation Time: 5 minutes
Cooking Time: 25 minutes

Nutrition Facts

Serving size:
1/4 of a
recipe (7.6
ounces).

Amount Per Serving	
Calories	160.93
Calories From Fat (7%)	11.18
	% Daily Value
Total Fat 1.28g	2%
Saturated Fat 0.22g	1%
Cholesterol 0.15mg	<1%
Sodium 119.97mg	5%
Potassium 327.27mg	9%
Total Carbohydrates 33.93g	11%
Fiber 3.9g	16%
Sugar 15.55g	
Protein 5.1g	10%

Sweet Potato and Pea Curry

1	cup	long grain brown rice	1	tsp	turmeric
1	tsp	cumin	2	tsp	grated lemon zest
1	tsp	coriander	1	(10 oz) package	frozen baby green peas, thawed
1	Tbsp	olive oil			
1/4	cup	chopped onion			
2	cloves	garlic minced	2	Tbsp	chopped fresh cilantro
2 1/2	cup	vegetable broth	1	pinch	sea salt
2	small	sweet potatoes peeled and cut into 1/4-inch cubes	1	pinch	black pepper

Procedure

1 Cook rice according to package directions.

2 In a small dry skillet. Place cumin and coriander and shake over medium heat until fragrant. Set aside.

3 Heat oil in a large saucepan. Add the onion and garlic and cook for 2 min. Add the broth and bring to a boil. Cover and lower heat to medium low. Cook the mixture until the potatoes are tender, about 12 to 15 min. Add lemon zest and peas. Cook, uncovered for 3 min. Add cilantro, salt and black pepper. Serve over rice.

Servings: 4
Yield: 4

Preparation Time: 10 minutes
Cooking Time: 30 minutes

Nutrition Facts

Serving size: 1/4 of a recipe (11.6 ounces).

Amount Per Serving	
Calories	270.85
Calories From Fat (6%)	15.44
	% Daily Value
Total Fat 1.84g	3%
Saturated Fat 0.35g	2%
Cholesterol 0mg	0%
Sodium 764.05mg	32%
Potassium 471.97mg	13%
Total Carbohydrates 57.52g	19%
Fiber 5.62g	22%
Sugar 6.99g	
Protein 6.59g	13%

Lunch

Black Bean Salad

1	(15 oz) can	black beans rinsed and drained	1	tsp dried oregano
1	small	yellow bell pepper chopped	1	tsp dried basil
1	small	red bell pepper chopped	1/2 tsp	ground cumin
1	small	tomato chopped	1/2	lime, juiced
1	cup	canned corn	1/4 tsp	salt
2		scallions chopped	1/4 tsp	black pepper
1	Tbsp	chopped fresh cilantro		

Procedure

1 Combine all ingredients in a salad bowl. Let sit for 30 minutes in the fridge to allow flavors to blend. Serve chilled or at room temperature.

Servings: 4
Yield: 4

Preparation Time: 15 minutes

Nutrition Facts

Serving size: 1/4 of a recipe (5.8 ounces).

Amount Per Serving	
Calories	207.43
Calories From Fat (2%)	3.8
	% Daily Value
Total Fat 0.45g	<1%
Saturated Fat 0.09g	<1%
Cholesterol 0mg	0%
Sodium 217.04mg	9%
Potassium 402.85mg	12%
Total Carbohydrates 46.12g	15%
Fiber 4.25g	17%
Sugar 1.66g	
Protein 4.91g	10%

Pinto Bean Cakes and Mango Salsa

Bean cakes:

1/2	cup	salsa
2	tsp	ground cumin
2	(15 oz) can	pinto beans , drained
1 1/2	cup	bread crumbs
1/4	cup	finely chopped scallions
1/2	tsp	salt
1/2	tsp	black pepper vegetable oil cooking spray

Salsa:

2		mangoes, peeled and cubed
1/4 cup		finely chopped red onion
1/4 cup		finely chopped red bell pepper
2	Tbsp	finely chopped scallions
2	Tbsp	finely chopped fresh cilantro
2	Tbsp	fresh lime juice
2	tsp	agave nectar
	pinch	cayenne pepper

Procedure

1. Preheat the oven to 200 degrees F. Combine the salsa, cumin and black beans in a food processor and pulse until smooth. Add 1 cup bread crumbs, scallions, salt and black pepper.

2. Divide the mixture into small patties, roughly 1/8 cup each. Dredge the patties in the remaining 1/2 cup bread crumbs. Set the patties on a tray and refrigerate for 30 min.

3. While the bean cakes chill, combine all salsa ingredients and refrigerate until serving time.

4. Heat a non stick large skillet over medium heat. Using cooking spray throughout the sauté process, sauté the cake for about 3 min per side, until lightly brown. Place the cakes on a baking sheet and place in the 200 degrees F oven until all cakes are prepared. Serve the cakes with the salsa.

Servings: 4
Yield: 4

Preparation Time: 30 minutes
Cooking Time: 30 minutes

Nutrition Facts

Serving size: 1/4 of a recipe (10.6 ounces).

Amount Per Serving	
Calories	368.91
Calories From Fat (8%)	30.59
	% Daily Value
Total Fat 3.53g	5%
Saturated Fat 0.76g	4%
Cholesterol 0mg	0%
Sodium 770.48mg	32%
Potassium 727.83mg	21%
Total Carbohydrates 72.27g	24%
Fiber 12.22g	49%
Sugar 20.35g	
Protein 14.96g	30%

Easy Chickpea Lunch

1/4 cup		vegetable broth	1/2 tsp	dried oregano
1	medium	onion chopped	1 (15 oz) can	chickpeas rinsed
3		plum tomato,		and drained
		peeled, seeded and	1/2 tsp	salt
		chopped	1/2 tsp	black pepper
2	cloves	garlic, minced		
1		bay leaf		

Procedure

1. Heat the broth in a skillet over medium high heat. Add onion and cooked for 5 min. Put in the tomatoes and garlic and cook for 3 min. Add the bay leaf and oregano. Lower heat, cover, and set heat to a low simmer for about 10 to 15 min.

2. Put in the chickpeas, salt and black pepper, and cook for an additional 5 min. or until chickpeas are heated through.

Servings: 6

Preparation Time: 10 minutes
Cooking Time: 25 minutes

Nutrition Facts

Serving size: 1/6 of a recipe (4 ounces).

Amount Per Serving	
Calories	65.8
Calories From Fat (8%)	5.01
	% Daily Value
Total Fat 0.61g	<1%
Saturated Fat 0.06g	<1%
Cholesterol 0mg	0%
Sodium 193.97mg	8%
Potassium 189.28mg	5%
Total Carbohydrates 13.18g	4%
Fiber 2.6g	10%
Sugar 0.88g	
Protein 2.59g	5%

Marseille Stew

2	Tbsp	olive oil	1/4 tsp		crushed red pepper
1	large	onion chopped			
2		garlic clove minced	1	(16 oz) can	white beans drained and rinsed
3	cups	peeled and cubed butternut squash			
3	cups	coarsely chopped green cabbage	1	cup	canned diced tomatoes
			1/2 tsp		salt
4	cups	vegetable broth	1/2 tsp		black pepper
1	Tbsp	chopped fresh thyme			

Procedure

1 Heat the oil in large saucepan over medium heat. add the onion and garlic and sauté for 5 min. Add the squash, cabbage, broth, thyme, and crushed red pepper and bring to boil.

2 Lower heat, cover and simmer on medium low for about 30 min, or until the squash is tender.

3 Add the beans and tomatoes, cover and continue to simmer 10 min. Season with salt and black pepper.

Servings: 4
Yield: 4

Preparation Time: 10 minutes
Cooking Time: 45 minutes

Nutrition Facts

Serving size: 1/4 of a recipe (20.6 ounces).

Amount Per Serving	
Calories	433.15
Calories From Fat (10%)	42.71
	% Daily Value
Total Fat 4.81g	7%
Saturated Fat 1.12g	6%
Cholesterol 2.61mg	<1%
Sodium 1910.13mg	80%
Potassium 1979.79mg	57%
Total Carbohydrates 81.22g	27%
Fiber 16.24g	65%
Sugar 7.48g	
Protein 21.05g	42%

Barbecue Tofu

For the Barbecue Sauce:

1	(8 oz) can	tomato paste
1/2 cup		agave nectar
1	tsp	liquid smoke
1	tsp	ground cinnamon
1	tsp	ground allspice
2	clove	garlic, minced
2	Tbsp	Bragg's liquid aminos
1	pinch	cayenne pepper

For the kabobs:

1	pound	extra firm tofu
4		wooden skewers, vegetable oil cooking spray

Procedure

1. Combine all sauce ingredients in a small saucepan. Bring to a boil. Lower heat to simmer and cook for 5 min., stirring regularly. Set aside.
2. Cut the tofu into ½ inch cubes. Skewer onto wooden skewers.
3. Coat grill rack with cooking spray. Preheat gas grill to a medium-high heat. When the grill is ready, add the tofu, baste with sauce and grill for 1 min. Turn the tofu and brush with more barbecue sauce. Cook for additional min., until the tofu is browned.

Servings: 4
Yield: 4

Preparation Time: 5 minutes
Cooking Time: 10 minutes

Nutrition Facts

Serving size: 1/4 of a recipe (7.5 ounces).

Amount Per Serving	
Calories	274.75
Calories From Fat (22%)	59.4
	% Daily Value
Total Fat 7.1g	11%
Saturated Fat 0.71g	4%
Cholesterol 0mg	0%
Sodium 364.44mg	15%
Potassium 617.01mg	18%
Total Carbohydrates 46.7g	16%
Fiber 2.81g	11%
Sugar 40.57g	
Protein 13.38g	27%

Rice and Bean Burgers

2	Tbsp	olive oil
1	small	onion chopped
1		garlic clove minced
1	tsp	chili powder
1/2	tsp	ground cumin
1/4	tsp	cayenne pepper
1	pinch	salt
1	pinch	black pepper
1	cup	canned pinto beans, dried and rinsed
1	cup	cooked brown basmati rice
3/4	cup	bread crumbs
1/4	cup	finely chopped fresh parsley
6	slices	cheddar cheese
		Vegetable oil cooking spray
6	whole	Ezekiel hamburger buns
1	large	tomato thinly sliced
6		lettuce leaves
2	tsp	mustard
2		pickles, sliced

Procedure

1 Heat the oil in a large skillet over medium heat. Add the onion and garlic and sauté for 4 min. Add the chili powder, cumin, cayenne, salt and black pepper. Add the beans and turn the heat to high. Mash beans coarsely as they cook over low heat for about 2 min.

2 Transfer the beans to a bowl. Add the rice, bread crumbs and parsley and stir until combined. Form into 6 patties, place them on a plate, and let rest in the refrigerator for about 30 min.

3 Heat a large skillet, preferably cast iron, over medium heat and coat it with cooking spray. Place the patties in the skillet and cook for about 4 min per side, until brown and heated through. Serve on buns with tomato, lettuce, pickles and mustard.

Servings: 6
Yield: 6

Preparation Time: 1 hour
Cooking Time: 10 minutes

Nutrition Facts

Serving size: 1/6 of a recipe (14.8 ounces).

Amount Per Serving	
Calories	363.48
Calories From Fat (29%)	105.63
	% Daily Value
Total Fat 12.11g	19%
Saturated Fat 6.49g	32%
Cholesterol 29.85mg	10%
Sodium 539.19mg	22%
Potassium 730.5mg	21%
Total Carbohydrates 48.48g	16%
Fiber 6.91g	28%
Sugar 3.99g	
Protein 16.98g	34%

Spinach, Beet and Orange Salad

For the Dressing:

4	Tbsp	rice vinegar
2	Tbsp	agave nectar
2	tsp	paprika
2	tsp	fresh ginger, grated
1/2	tsp	chili powder

1		lime, juiced

For the Salad:

1/2	can	beets (plain, unpickled)
6	cups	baby spinach
2		mandarin oranges

Procedure

1 Whisk the vinegar, agave nectar, paprika, ginger, and chili powder in a saucepan and bring to a boil. Add lime juice. Let dressing cool.

2 Arrange spinach on a platter and top with beets and oranges. Drizzle dressing over the spinach salad.

Servings: 4

Preparation Time: 20 minutes
Cooking Time: 1 hour and 20 minutes

Nutrition Facts

Serving size: 1/4 of a recipe (16.3 ounces).

Amount Per Serving	
Calories	205.33
Calories From Fat (18%)	37.36
	% Daily Value
Total Fat 5.01g	8%
Saturated Fat 2.58g	13%
Cholesterol 18mg	6%
Sodium 237.54mg	10%
Potassium 1069.01mg	31%
Total Carbohydrates 44.03g	15%
Fiber 9.28g	37%
Sugar 21.83g	
Protein 10.41g	21%

Strawberry and Feta Salad

1	cup	slivered almonds	2	Tbsp	agave nectar
2		cloves garlic -- minced	1/2 cup		olive oil
1	tsp	Dijon mustard	1		head romaine lettuce, torn
1/4 cup		raspberry vinegar			
2	Tbsp	balsamic vinegar	1	pint	fresh strawberries, sliced
			1	cup	crumbled feta cheese

Procedure

1. In a skillet over medium-high heat, cook the almonds, stirring frequently, until lightly toasted. Remove from heat, and set aside.
2. Place the garlic, Dijon mustard, raspberry vinegar, balsamic vinegar, agave and olive oil in a blender and blend for 15 seconds.
3. In a large bowl, toss together the toasted almonds, romaine lettuce, strawberries, and feta cheese. Cover with the dressing mixture, and toss to serve.

Servings: 10

Preparation Time: 15 minutes
Total Time: 15 minutes

Nutrition Facts

Serving size: 1/10 of a recipe (6.9 ounces).

Amount Per Serving	
Calories	270.18
Calories From Fat (70%)	187.95
	% Daily Value
Total Fat 21.73g	33%
Saturated Fat 3.64g	18%
Cholesterol 13.35mg	4%
Sodium 181.57mg	8%
Potassium 403.25mg	12%
Total Carbohydrates 15.69g	5%
Fiber 4.48g	18%
Sugar 9.18g	
Protein 6.43g	13%

Strawberry Feta Salad II

2	Tbsp	sesame seeds	1/4	tsp	Worcestershire sauce
1	Tbsp	poppy seeds			
1/2	cup	agave nectar	1	Tbsp	minced onion
1/2	cup	olive oil	10	ounces	fresh spinach rinsed, dried and torn into bite size pieces
1/4	cup	distilled white vinegar			
1/4	tsp	paprika			
			1	quart	strawberries clean, hulled and sliced
			1/4	cup	almonds, blanched and slivered
			1	cup	feta cheese

Procedure

1. In a medium bowl, whisk together the sesame seeds, poppy seeds, agave, olive oil, vinegar, paprika, Worcestershire sauce and onion. Cover, and chill for one hour.

2. In a large bowl, combine the spinach, strawberries and almonds. Pour dressing over salad, and toss. Refrigerate 10 to 15 minutes before serving.

Servings: 4
Yield: 4

Preparation Time: 10 minutes plus 1 hr resting time
Total Time: 1 hour and 10 minutes

Nutrition Facts

Serving size: 1/4 of a recipe (8.2 ounces).

Amount Per Serving	
Calories	555.19
Calories From Fat (68%)	375.26
	% Daily Value
Total Fat 43.02g	66%
Saturated Fat 10.14g	51%
Cholesterol 33.34mg	11%
Sodium 479.98mg	20%
Potassium 600.33mg	17%
Total Carbohydrates 36.78g	12%
Fiber 4.31g	17%
Sugar 29.29g	
Protein 10.66g	21%

Snacks, Dips and Desserts

Basil Pesto Spread

1 cup	fresh basil leaves, chopped	1 pinch	salt
		1 pinch	black pepper
2 cloves	garlic chopped		
1 (12.3 oz) package	firm low fat silken tofu		

Procedure

1 Place all ingredients in a food processor and process until smooth.

Yield: 1 1/2 cups

Preparation Time: 5 minutes

Nutrition Facts

Serving size: Entire recipe (5.8 ounces).

Amount Per Serving	
Calories	209.84
Calories From Fat (15%)	31.04
	% Daily Value
Total Fat 3.66g	6%
Saturated Fat 1.68g	8%
Cholesterol 0mg	0%
Sodium 409.32mg	17%
Potassium 1981.82mg	57%
Total Carbohydrates 37.81g	13%
Fiber 27.48g	110%
Sugar 1.67g	
Protein 22.31g	45%

Cheesy Popcorn

2   Tbsp vegetable oil   1 Tbsp nutritional yeast
1/2 cup   popcorn kernel

Procedure

1 Heat oil in a large, covered pan over medium heat with 3 popcorn kernels. When first kernel pops, add the rest of the kernels. Shake the pan gently as the kernels pop. When popping decreases to a 2 or 3 second gap, remove from heat.

2 Transfer the popcorn to large bowl. Sprinkle with nutritional yeast and toss to mix.

Servings: 4

Preparation Time: 5 minutes

Nutrition Facts

Serving size: 1/4 of a recipe (0.4 ounces).

Amount Per Serving	
Calories	75.17
Calories From Fat (84%)	63.26
	% Daily Value
Total Fat 7.15g	11%
Saturated Fat 0.54g	3%
Cholesterol 0mg	0%
Sodium 0.25mg	<1%
Potassium 9.71mg	<1%
Total Carbohydrates 2.59g	<1%
Fiber 0.45g	2%
Sugar 0.03g	
Protein 0.39g	<1%

Chocolate Cherry Dessert

This dessert is nutritious, but fairly high in fruit sugar. Eat for dessert after a protein rich meal, like a fish dish.

1	cup	frozen cherries	3/4 cup milk
1		bananas	

Procedure

1 Put all ingredients into a blender and blend until smooth.

Servings: 4

Preparation Time: 5 minutes

Nutrition Facts

Serving size: 1/4 of a recipe (4 ounces).

Amount Per Serving	
Calories	66.96
Calories From Fat (15%)	10.35
	% Daily Value
Total Fat 1.17g	2%
Saturated Fat 0.65g	3%
Cholesterol 3.66mg	1%
Sodium 22.19mg	<1%
Potassium 217.71mg	6%
Total Carbohydrates 13.2g	4%
Fiber 1.39g	6%
Sugar 9.42g	
Protein 2.19g	4%

Creamy Fruit Smoothie

2	cups	milk	2	Tbsp	flax seeds
1 1/2	cup	fresh blue berries	1	Tbsp	agave nectar
1	large	banana			

Procedure

1. Combine all ingredients in a blender and blend until smooth and flaxseeds are ground.

Servings: 4
Yield: 4

Preparation Time: 5 minutes

Nutrition Facts

Serving size: 1/4 of a recipe (7.7 ounces).

Amount Per Serving	
Calories	154.23
Calories From Fat (22%)	34.67
	% Daily Value
Total Fat 3.97g	6%
Saturated Fat 1.7g	9%
Cholesterol 9.76mg	3%
Sodium 59.33mg	2%
Potassium 361.51mg	10%
Total Carbohydrates 26.69g	9%
Fiber 3.02g	12%
Sugar 20.1g	
Protein 5.36g	11%

Curry Chickpea Spread

Serve with whole grain crackers or dip carrots into the spread. Make sure to overload; you want fewer crackers and more dip!

2	Tbsp	olive oil	3 Tbsp	freshly squeezed lime juice
1	medium	onion, sliced	1 1/4 tsp	kosher salt
3	cloves	garlic	1/8 tsp	freshly ground black pepper
2	(15 oz) can	chickpeas rinsed and drained		
1	Tbsp	curry powder		

Procedure

1. Sauté onion and garlic for about 5 minutes in olive oil over medium heat until lightly browned.
2. Add the onion, garlic, the remaining ingredients and 1/4 cup water to a food processor and process until smooth.

Servings: 3
Yield: 3 cups

Preparation Time: 35 minutes

Nutrition Facts

Serving size: 1/3 of a recipe (7.7 ounces).

Amount Per Serving	
Calories	220.43
Calories From Fat (8%)	18.28
	% Daily Value
Total Fat 2.18g	3%
Saturated Fat 0.26g	1%
Cholesterol 0mg	0%
Sodium 1265.13mg	53%
Potassium 392.32mg	11%
Total Carbohydrates 43.16g	14%
Fiber 8.51g	34%
Sugar 1.9g	
Protein 8.85g	18%

Fresh Blueberry Pie

11/3	cup	pitted dates
1 1/2	Tbsp	orange juice
2	cups	graham cracker crumbs, coarsely crushed
2	Tbsp	agave nectar
3 1/2	cup	blueberries
1/4	tsp	ground cinnamon

2	cups	strawberries, sliced

Banana Cashew Cream

1/4		banana
1/4	cup	raw cashews, soaked for at least 6 hours

Procedure

1. Puree the dates and orange juice in a food processor or blender.
2. Mash the date puree and graham cracker crumbs together with your hands to combine. Pat the crust into a glass pie dish.
3. Stir together the agave nectar, berries and cinnamon. Add the remaining date puree, and sliced strawberries. Spread the mixture in the pie dish and refrigerate for 2 hours.
4. Top each slice with a dollop of Banana Cashew Cream.
5. To make the Banana Cashew Cream: Blend the banana and cashews with 2 tbsp water in a food processor or blender until creamy. Refrigerate until ready to use.

Servings: 8

Preparation Time: 2 hours and 20 minutes

Nutrition Facts

Serving size: 1/8 of a recipe (3.5 ounces).

Amount Per Serving	
Calories	136.36
Calories From Fat (31%)	42.16
	% Daily Value
Total Fat 5g	8%
Saturated Fat 1.26g	6%
Cholesterol 0mg	0%
Sodium 11.27mg	<1%
Potassium 249.86mg	7%
Total Carbohydrates 23.41g	8%
Fiber 2.55g	10%
Sugar 16.78g	
Protein 2.34g	5%

Tomatillo and Cilantro Salsa

This makes a wonderful dip. Serve with warm queso cheese and tortilla chips. Make sure to overload with the cheese to ensure a good protein balance.

1	small	red onion chopped	1 cup		packed cilantro leaves and tender stems
1 1/2	pound	fresh tomatillos, husks removed, chopped	1		lime, juiced
2		jalapeño pepper, stems and seeds removed, chopped	1 tsp		salt

Procedure

1. Process all ingredients in a food processor until smooth.

Yield: 4 1/2 cups

Preparation Time: 5 minutes

Nutrition Facts

Serving size: Entire recipe (39 ounces).

Amount Per Serving	
Calories	346.65
Calories From Fat (18%)	63.38
	% Daily Value
Total Fat 7.54g	12%
Saturated Fat 0.98g	5%
Cholesterol 0mg	0%
Sodium 1939.27mg	81%
Potassium 2539.39mg	73%
Total Carbohydrates 69.84g	23%
Fiber 18.04g	72%
Sugar 44.77g	
Protein 10.43g	21%

Fruit Kabobs and Vanilla Peach Dip

1	cup	seedless grapes	2	(6 oz) container peach flavored yogurt, low fat
1	cup	chopped fresh mango		
2		mandarin oranges, peeled and segmented	1 tsp	vanilla extract
1		apple, chopped	2 tsp	ground cinnamon
				Toothpicks

Procedure

1 Mix the yogurt, vanilla and cinnamon.
2 Skewer the fruit with the toothpicks and dip in the yogurt.

Servings: 6

Preparation Time: 5 minutes

Nutrition Facts

Serving size: 1/6 of a recipe (5.3 ounces).

Amount Per Serving	
Calories	67.51
Calories From Fat (3%)	2.09
	% Daily Value
Total Fat 0.24g	<1%
Saturated Fat 0.05g	<1%
Cholesterol 0mg	0%
Sodium 47.19mg	2%
Potassium 194.16mg	6%
Total Carbohydrates 14.57g	5%
Fiber 1.96g	8%
Sugar 11.7g	
Protein 2.45g	5%

Guacamole

3		avocados peeled, pitted and mashed	3	Tbsp	chopped fresh cilantro
1		lime juice	2		roma (plum) tomatoes, diced
1	tsp	salt	1	tsp	minced garlic
1/2 cup		diced red onion	1	pinch	ground cayenne pepper

Procedure

1 In a medium bowl, mash together the avocados, lime juice, and salt. Mix in onion, cilantro, tomatoes, and garlic. Stir in cayenne pepper. Refrigerate 1 hour for best flavor, or serve immediately.

Servings: 4
Yield: 4

Preparation Time: 10 minutes
Total Time: 10 minutes

Nutrition Facts

Serving size: 1/4 of a recipe (8.7 ounces).

Amount Per Serving	
Calories	263.74
Calories From Fat (71%)	186.27
	% Daily Value
Total Fat 22.27g	34%
Saturated Fat 3.23g	16%
Cholesterol 0mg	0%
Sodium 596.95mg	25%
Potassium 934.57mg	27%
Total Carbohydrates 17.98g	6%
Fiber 11.32g	45%
Sugar 3.69g	
Protein 3.92g	8%

Peach Smoothie

2	cups	milk	2	Tbsp	flax seeds
1	cup	chopped fresh peaches	1	Tbsp	agave nectar
1/4	tsp	almond extract			

Procedure

1 Combine all ingredients in a blender and blend until smooth and the flax seeds are ground.

Servings: 4

Preparation Time: 5 minutes

Nutrition Facts

Serving size: 1/4 of a recipe (6.2 ounces).

Amount Per Serving	
Calories	125.97
Calories From Fat (35%)	43.86
	% Daily Value
Total Fat 5.05g	8%
Saturated Fat 1.76g	9%
Cholesterol 9.76mg	3%
Sodium 59.35mg	2%
Potassium 303.06mg	9%
Total Carbohydrates 15.97g	5%
Fiber 2.29g	9%
Sugar 14.14g	
Protein 5.53g	11%

Pickled Onions

Finding alternatives to snacks can be a challenge for reactive hypoglycemia, especially when many brands of pickle have added sugar. This pickling sauce has a very small amount of sugar and can be used for other vegetables, if you don't like onions.

1/2	cup	pickling salt (do not substitute regular table salt)	1/4 tsp		ground allspice
			1/4 tsp		hot pepper flakes
2	quarts	water	1		bay leaf crumbled
1 1/2	pound	pearl onions, peeled and steamed until tender	2	Tbsp	snipped fresh chives
2	Tbsp	brown sugar			
3	cups	cider vinegar			
1	tsp	black peppercorns, crushed roughly in a mortar and pestle			

Procedure

1. Dissolve 1/4 cup salt in 1 quart water in a glass bowl. Add the onions. Weight them gently with a plate that fits inside the bowl (I used a can on a saucer). Let them stand overnight

2. Drain and then peel the onions. Remove tips of onions (leave the root end intact) with a sharp knife. Place back in the bowl. Make another brine with the remaining 1/4 cup pickling salt and water, pour it over the onions, and then weight them gently again. Let them stand for 2 days in the refrigerator.

3. Bring the sugar and vinegar to a boil in a saucepan. Stir to dissolve and then let the liquid cool to room temperature.

4. Drain and rinse the onions well. In a 1- quart Mason jar, layer the onions, peppercorns, allspice, pepper flakes, bay leaf and chives. Cover them with the cooled, sweetened vinegar. Cover the jar.

5. Refrigerate the jar for at least 3 weeks before eating. They will keep for up to six months.

Servings: 40
Yield: 1 quart

Nutrition Facts

Serving size: 1/40 of a recipe (1.8 ounces).

Amount Per Serving	
Calories	2.93
Calories From Fat (2%)	0.05
	% Daily Value
Total Fat 0.01g	<1%
Saturated Fat 0g	0%
Cholesterol 0mg	0%
Sodium 1.65mg	<1%
Potassium 3.37mg	<1%
Total Carbohydrates 0.75g	<1%
Fiber 0.03g	<1%
Sugar 0.67g	
Protein 0.02g	<1%

Pico De Gallo

1	large	sweet onion, chopped
15	(about 2 pounds)	roma (plum) tomatoes, chopped
2		jalapeño peppers, seeded and chopped
1	cup	cilantro, chopped
1	tsp	salt
2	Tbsp	lemon juice

Procedure

1 Mix all ingredients together in a large bowl and serve.

Servings: 7
Yield: 7

Preparation Time: 20 minutes

Nutrition Facts

Serving size: 1/7 of a recipe (15.8 ounces).

Amount Per Serving	
Calories	88.26
Calories From Fat (8%)	7.32
	% Daily Value
Total Fat 0.87g	1%
Saturated Fat 0.11g	<1%
Cholesterol 0mg	0%
Sodium 295.35mg	12%
Potassium 1018.34mg	29%
Total Carbohydrates 19.42g	6%
Fiber 5.36g	21%
Sugar 12.79g	
Protein 3.96g	8%

Spinach Dip

2	Tbsp	olive oil	1 tsp	ground coriander
1	small	onion quartered	1 1/2 tsp	salt
4	cloves	garlic	1/4 tsp	black pepper
			pinch	cayenne pepper

2 Tbsp olive oil

1 small onion quartered

4 cloves garlic

1 (10 oz) package frozen chopped spinach, thawed

1 (12.3 oz) package firm silken tofu

1 Tbsp lemon juice

1 tsp ground coriander

1 1/2 tsp salt

1/4 tsp black pepper

pinch cayenne pepper

Procedure

1 Saute onion and garlic in the olive oil until soft, about 4-5 minutes.

2 Place the spinach in a clean dish towel. Squeeze and twist the dish towel to press out water from the spinach.

3 Place the spinach, onions, and garlic in a food processor and process until well chopped. Add the remaining ingredients and process until smooth.

Yield: 2 1/2 cups

Preparation Time: 35 minutes

Nutrition Facts

Serving size: Entire recipe (12.2 ounces).

Amount Per Serving	
Calories	132.59
Calories From Fat (14%)	18
	% Daily Value
Total Fat 2.08g	3%
Saturated Fat 0.25g	1%
Cholesterol 0mg	0%
Sodium 3012.6mg	126%
Potassium 790.76mg	23%
Total Carbohydrates 20.44g	7%
Fiber 6.93g	28%
Sugar 4.88g	
Protein 12.83g	26%

Soup

African Peanut Soup

1	tablespoon	olive oil	1/2 teaspoon	curry powder
1	large	skinless, boneless chicken breast halves (4 oz. each)	1/2 teaspoon	ground cumin
			1/4 teaspoon	chili powder
			1/4 teaspoon	cayenne pepper
			1/4 teaspoon	crushed red pepper flakes
1/2		onion chopped	1/4 teaspoon	ground cinnamon
1		red bell pepper, sliced	1/4 teaspoon	ground black pepper
2		Clove garlic -- minced	1/2 cup	brown rice
			1/2 cup	crunchy peanut butter
1	14 ounce	crushed tomatoes		
1		sweet potato peeled and cut into bite size pieces		
1 1/2 cups		sliced carrots		
8	cups	chicken broth or more as needed		

Procedure

1 Heat olive oil in a skillet over medium heat, and brown the chicken breasts on both sides, about 5 minutes per side. Place the chicken breasts into a slow cooker. Cook the onion, red bell peppers, and garlic in the hot skillet until the onions are translucent, about 5 minutes; transfer the cooked vegetables into the slow cooker.

2 Stir the crushed tomatoes, sweet potatoes, carrots, chicken broth, curry powder, cumin, chili powder, cayenne pepper, red pepper flakes, cinnamon, and black pepper into the slow cooker. Set the cooker to High, and cook for 5 to 6 hours, or cook on Low for 10 hours. Stir in additional chicken broth throughout the cooking time if needed.

3 Mix in the brown rice 3 hours before serving, and mix in the peanut butter at least 1 hour before serving. Shred chicken meat, and serve hot.

Servings: 20
Yield: 20

Preparation Time: 30 minutes
Cooking Time: 5 hours
Total Time: 5 hours and 30 minutes

Nutrition Facts

Serving size: 1/20 of a recipe (3.5 ounces).

Amount Per Serving	
Calories	202
Calories From Fat (35%)	16.31
	% Daily Value
Total Fat 8.6g	13%
Saturated Fat 1.4g	7%
Cholesterol 13mg	4%
Sodium 161mg	7%
Potassium 502mg	14%
Total Carbohydrates 22.6g	8%
Fiber 4g	16%
Sugar 4.3g	
Protein 10.6g	21%

Quick Black Bean Soup

2	(15 oz) can	black beans, drained and rinsed	1	tsp	ground cumin
			4	Tbsp	sour cream
			2	Tbsp	thinly sliced green onion
1 1/2 cup		vegetable broth	1		Roma tomato, chopped
1	cup	salsa			

Procedure

1 Combine beans, broth, salsa, and cumin in a blender. Blend until fairly smooth.

2 Heat the bean mixture in a saucepan over medium heat until thoroughly heated.

3 Ladle soup into 4 individual bowls, and top each bowl with sour cream, green onion and tomato.

Servings: 4
Yield: 4

Preparation Time: 10 minutes
Cooking Time: 10 minutes
Total Time: 20 minutes

Nutrition Facts

Serving size: 1/4 of a recipe (9.1 ounces).

Amount Per Serving	
Calories	218.02
Calories From Fat (18%)	39.42
	% Daily Value
Total Fat 4.49g	7%
Saturated Fat 1.86g	9%
Cholesterol 7.16mg	2%
Sodium 1213.07mg	51%
Potassium 677.37mg	19%
Total Carbohydrates 35.12g	12%
Fiber 9.85g	39%
Sugar 2.49g	
Protein 11.25g	22%

Orange Black Bean Soup

2 tbsp		olive oil	pinch	crushed red pepper
3		garlic cloves finely chopped	1	bay leaf
1 1/4 cup		chopped red onions	1/2 cup	pulp free orange juice
2	cups	vegetable broth		kosher or sea salt to taste
1	tsp	ground cumin		Freshly ground black pepper to taste
1	tsp	dried oregano	1/4 cup	chopped fresh cilantro
2	(15 oz) can	black beans, with liquid		

Procedure

1 Saute the garlic and onions in the olive oil over medium heat until brown, about 5 min. Add the cumin and oregano and cook for 1 min.

2 Add the beans with their liquid, the vegetable broth, crush red pepper and bay leaf. Bring the soup to a boil, lower the heat and simmer, uncovered for 20 min. stirring occasionally. Add the orange juice, salt and black pepper.

3 Remove the bay leaf. Puree half the bean mixture in a blender or food processor and add back to the soup. Serve each bowl garnished with cilantro.

Servings: 5
Yield: 5

Preparation Time: 10 minutes
Cooking Time: 35 minutes

Nutrition Facts

Serving size: 1/5 of a recipe (8.8 ounces).

Amount Per Serving	
Calories	194.88
Calories From Fat (10%)	20.16
	% Daily Value
Total Fat 2.29g	4%
Saturated Fat 0.52g	3%
Cholesterol 1.11mg	<1%
Sodium 957.12mg	40%
Potassium 492.29mg	14%
Total Carbohydrates 35.3g	12%
Fiber 8.38g	34%
Sugar 2.8g	
Protein 9.5g	19%

Vegetable Soup

5	cups	vegetable broth	1	(15 oz) can	tomatoes, chopped
1/2	cup	quick-cooking brown rice	2	tsp	dried basil
1	(15 oz) can	chickpeas rinsed and drained	1	tsp	dried oregano
1		carrot, chopped			kosher or sea salt to taste
1/2	cup	peas			Freshly ground black pepper to taste
1/2	cup	small cauliflower florets			

Procedure

1. Bring the broth to a boil in a large saucepan. Add chickpeas, carrot, peas, cauliflower, tomatoes, basil and oregano and simmer for 15 to 20 min.

2. Add the brown rice. Cover, reduce heat to low and cook for 10 min. Season with salt and black pepper.

Servings: 6
Yield: 6

Preparation Time: 10 minutes
Cooking Time: 30 minutes

Nutrition Facts

Serving size: 1/6 of a recipe (11 ounces).

Amount Per Serving	
Calories	129.19
Calories From Fat (7%)	9.06
	% Daily Value
Total Fat 1.09g	2%
Saturated Fat 0.08g	<1%
Cholesterol 0mg	0%
Sodium 638.81mg	27%
Potassium 218.65mg	6%
Total Carbohydrates 28.35g	9%
Fiber 3.93g	16%
Sugar 3.28g	
Protein 3.69g	7%

Squash and Sweet Potato Soup

2 Tbsp	unsalted butter	1	Tbsp	grated fresh ginger root
1 cup	diced onion			
6 cups	butternut squash peeled, seeded and cut into 1/2-inch cubes	1	tsp	ground turmeric
		1/2	tsp	ground coriander
		1/4	tsp	ground black pepper
4 1/2	cups sweet potatoes peeled and cut into 1/2-inch cubes	1		green chili peppers, halved lengthwise (optional)
6 cups	vegetable broth	1	cup	silken tofu, divided
3 Tbsp	chopped fresh thyme	1/2	tsp	salt

Procedure

1 Melt the butter in a large stock pot over medium heat. Stir in the onion; cook and stir until the onion has softened and turned translucent, about 5 minutes. Add the butternut squash, sweet potatoes, and enough vegetable broth to cover. Stir in the thyme, ginger, turmeric, coriander, black pepper, and chili pepper. Bring to a boil over medium-high heat, and then reduce heat to medium-low. Cover and simmer until vegetables are very tender, 20 to 30 minutes, stirring occasionally.

2 Puree soup with a hand blender until smooth.

Servings: 6
Yield: 6

Preparation Time: 35 minutes
Cooking Time: 30 minutes
Total Time: 1 hour and 5 minutes

Nutrition Facts

Serving size: 1/6 of a recipe (17.5 ounces).

Amount Per Serving	
Calories	322.88
Calories From Fat (23%)	73.18
	% Daily Value
Total Fat 8.27g	13%
Saturated Fat 3.43g	17%
Cholesterol 12.64mg	4%
Sodium 1789.83mg	75%
Potassium 1131.83mg	32%
Total Carbohydrates 55.9g	19%
Fiber 8.43g	34%
Sugar 6.19g	
Protein 9.68g	19%

Cajun Bean Soup

4	slices	vegetarian bacon	1/2 tsp		dried thyme
2	tbsp	olive oil	1/4 tsp		crushed red pepper
5	cups	vegetable broth			
4	small	carrots thinly sliced	½ tsp		salt
			½ tsp		black pepper
1	medium	onion, chopped	2	(15 oz) can	great Northern Beans
3		garlic cloves, minced	2	cups	chopped fresh spinach
1/2	tsp	dried oregano			
1/2	tsp	dried basil			

Procedure

1 Cook vegetarian bacon in a non stick skillet over medium-high heat until crisp. Crumble and set aside.

2 In a large saucepan, heat the oil over medium heat. Add the carrots, onion and garlic and sauté for 5 min. Add the broth, oregano, basil, thyme, crushed red pepper, salt, black pepper, and beans. Bring to a boil, reduce heat to low and simmer for about 5 min.

3 Puree soup with a hand blender. Add spinach and cook 1 minute until the spinach is wilted. Stir bacon into the soup.

Servings: 6
Yield: 6

Preparation Time: 10 minutes
Cooking Time: 20 minutes

Nutrition Facts

Serving size: 1/6 of a recipe (12.4 ounces).

Amount Per Serving	
Calories	357.39
Calories From Fat (37%)	131.32
	% Daily Value
Total Fat 14.63g	23%
Saturated Fat 4.56g	23%
Cholesterol 18.97mg	6%
Sodium 1445.41mg	60%
Potassium 835.42mg	24%
Total Carbohydrates 43.23g	14%
Fiber 8.21g	33%
Sugar 2.42g	
Protein 14.55g	29%

Cauliflower Chowder

2	tbsp	olive oil	1		bay leaf
3	cups	vegetable broth	1 cup		2% milk
4	large	shallots, minced	2 Tbsp		finely chopped fresh basil
1/2	cup	chopped celery	½ tsp		salt
6	cups	cauliflower florets (about 1 medium head)	½ tsp		black pepper
1	cup	chopped red bell pepper			
1	medium	sweet potato, peeled and cut into 1/4 inch cubes			

Procedure

1. Heat the oil over medium heat. Add the shallots and celery and sauté for 5min. Add the broth and 1 cup water and bring to boil. Add the cauliflower, bell pepper, sweet potato and bay leaf and bring to a boil.
2. Reduce the heat, cover and simmer for 20 min. Remove the bay leaf.
3. Add the milk. For a heartier consistency, puree half the soup. Add the basil and season with salt and black pepper.

Servings: 6
Yield: 6

Preparation Time: 20 minutes
Cooking Time: 35 minutes

Nutrition Facts

Serving size: 1/6 of a recipe (11.6 ounces).

Amount Per Serving	
Calories	167.39
Calories From Fat (18%)	29.39
	% Daily Value
Total Fat 3.31g	5%
Saturated Fat 1.1g	6%
Cholesterol 4.59mg	2%
Sodium 999.67mg	42%
Potassium 761.79mg	22%
Total Carbohydrates 28.8g	10%
Fiber 5.48g	22%
Sugar 5.75g	
Protein 7.58g	15%

Cream of Asparagus Soup

3	cups	sliced asparagus		pinch	ground nutmeg
2	cups	vegetable broth	1	tsp	salt
3/4	tsp	chopped fresh thyme	1/4	tsp	grated lemon zest
1		bay leaf	1/2	Tbsp	lemon juice
1		garlic clove, crushed	½	tsp	black pepper to taste
2	Tbsp	rice flour	½	tsp	hot sauce
2	cups	milk			

Procedure

1. Combine asparagus, broth, 1/2 tsp thyme, bay leaf and garlic in a large saucepan over medium high heat. Bring to a boil. Cover, reduce heat, and simmer for 10 min. Discard the bay leaf. Place the asparagus mixture in a blender, cover and puree until smooth.

2. Place the flour in a large sauce pan over medium heat. Gradually add the milk, stirring with a whisk until blended. Add the pureed asparagus mixture and nutmeg and stir to combine. Bring to a boil. Reduced heat and simmer for 5 min. Remove from heat and strain. Add the remaining 1/4 tsp thyme, salt, lemon juice, lemon zest and black pepper. Add hot sauce and stir.

Servings: 4
Yield: 4

Preparation Time: 5 minutes
Cooking Time: 35 minutes

Nutrition Facts

Serving size: 1/4 of a recipe (19.9 ounces).

Amount Per Serving	
Calories	180.13
Calories From Fat (18%)	31.56
	% Daily Value
Total Fat 3.61g	6%
Saturated Fat 0.61g	3%
Cholesterol 1.23mg	<1%
Sodium 2462.98mg	103%
Potassium 902.66mg	26%
Total Carbohydrates 28.41g	9%
Fiber 5.72g	23%
Sugar 3.17g	
Protein 12.32g	25%

Cream of Chicken Soup with Wild Rice

4	cups	chicken broth	1/2	tsp	ground black pepper
2	cups	water	3/4	cup	all purpose flour
2	halves	cooked, boneless chicken breast, shredded	1/2	cup	butter
			1 1/2	cup	milk
			1/2	cup	heavy cream
1	(4.5 oz) package	quick cooking long grain and wild rice with seasoning packet			
1/2 tsp		salt			

Procedure

1 In a large pot over medium heat, combine broth, water and chicken. Bring just to boiling, then stir in rice, reserving seasoning packet. Cover and remove from heat.

2 In a small bowl, combine salt, pepper and flour. In a medium saucepan over medium heat, melt butter. Stir in contents of seasoning packet until mixture is bubbly. Reduce heat to low, then stir in flour mixture by tablespoons, to form a roux. Whisk in cream, a little at a time, until fully incorporated and smooth. Cook until thickened, 5 minutes.

3 Stir cream mixture and milk into broth and rice. Cook over medium heat until heated through, 10 to 15 minutes.

Servings: 8
Yield: 8

Preparation Time: 5 minutes
Cooking Time: 20 minutes
Total Time: 25 minutes

Nutrition Facts

Serving size: 1/8 of a recipe (10.8 ounces).

Amount Per Serving	
Calories	270.3
Calories From Fat (56%)	152.4
	% Daily Value
Total Fat 17.23g	27%
Saturated Fat 10.15g	51%
Cholesterol 74.15mg	25%
Sodium 566.38mg	24%
Potassium 280.76mg	8%
Total Carbohydrates 11.9g	4%
Fiber 0.35g	1%
Sugar 2.71g	
Protein 16.29g	33%

Fish and Tamarind Soup

1	Tbsp	olive oil	6	cups	water
8		shallots chopped	6	tsp	lemon grass powder
6		cloves garlic crushed	1/4 cup		tamarind juice
1/2 tsp		crushed red pepper	¼ tsp		salt
1/2 tsp		ground turmeric	2	pounds	red snapper fillets, cut into 1 inch pieces

Procedure

1. Heat oil in a large saucepan over medium heat. Mix in shallots, garlic, crushed red pepper, and turmeric. Cook and stir until shallots are tender, about 5 minutes. Pour water into skillet, and mix in lemon grass and tamarind juice. Season with salt. Bring the mixture to a boil.

2. Stir snapper into boiling mixture. Cook 10 minutes, or until fish pieces are easily flaked with a fork.

Servings: 6
Yield: 6

Preparation Time: 15 minutes
Cooking Time: 15 minutes
Total Time: 30 minutes

Nutrition Facts

Serving size: 1/6 of a recipe (34.9 ounces).

Amount Per Serving	
Calories	472.24
Calories From Fat (6%)	28.06
	% Daily Value
Total Fat 3.22g	5%
Saturated Fat 0.35g	2%
Cholesterol 0mg	0%
Sodium 123.52mg	5%
Potassium 2266.97mg	65%
Total Carbohydrates 106.77g	36%
Fiber 0.1g	<1%
Sugar 0.04g	
Protein 14.62g	29%

Chinese Mushroom Soup

1	oz	dried wood ear mushrooms	1	quart	chicken broth
4		dried shiitake mushrooms	1/4 tsp		crushed red pepper flakes
12		dried tiger lily buds	1/2 tsp		ground black pepper
2	cups	hot water	3/4 tsp		ground white pepper
1/3 oz		bamboo fungus	1/2 Tbsp		chili oil
3	Tbsp	Bragg's liquid aminos	1/2 Tbsp		sesame oil
5	Tbsp	rice vinegar	1		green onion sliced
1/4 cup		corn starch	1	cup	Chinese dried mushrooms
1	(8 oz)	container firm tofu, cut into 1/4 inch cubes			

Procedure

1. In a small bowl, place wood mushrooms, shiitake mushrooms, and lily buds in 1 1/2 cups hot water. Soak 20 minutes, until rehydrated. Drain, reserving liquid. Trim stems from the mushrooms, and cut into thin strips. Cut the lily buds in half.

2. In a separate small bowl, soak bamboo fungus in 1/4 cup lightly salted hot water. Soak about 20 minutes, until rehydrated. Drain, mince and add to mushroom mixture.

3. In a third small bowl, blend Bragg's, rice vinegar, and 1 tablespoon cornstarch. Place 1/2 the tofu cubes into the mixture.

4. In a medium saucepan, mix the reserved mushroom and lily bud liquid with the vegetable broth. Bring to a boil, and stir in the wood mushrooms, shiitake mushrooms, lily buds and fungus. Season with red pepper, black pepper, and white pepper.

5. Reduce heat, and simmer 3 to 5 minutes.

6. Rinse one of the small bowls, then mix remaining cornstarch and remaining water. Stir into the broth mixture until thickened.

7. Mix Bragg's mixture and remaining tofu strips into the saucepan. Return to boil, and stir in the chili oil and sesame oil. Garnish with green onion to serve.

Servings: 4

Yield: 4

Preparation Time: 45 minutes
Cooking Time: 15 minutes
Total Time: 1 hour

Nutrition Facts

Serving size: 1/4 of a recipe (27.1 ounces).

Amount Per Serving	
Calories	251.45
Calories From Fat (22%)	54.65
	% Daily Value
Total Fat 6.93g	11%
Saturated Fat 1.26g	6%
Cholesterol 2.46mg	<1%
Sodium 2034.62mg	85%
Potassium 643.03mg	18%
Total Carbohydrates 46.48g	15%
Fiber 4.15g	17%
Sugar 0.49g	
Protein 9.33g	19%

Thai Mushroom Soup

4 1/2	cup	chicken broth	2	cups	Shiitake mushrooms, stems removed, thinly sliced
1	large	shallot finely chopped			
2	cloves	garlic, thinly sliced	2	Tbsp	Bragg's liquid aminos
			1	Tbsp	dry sherry
1	tsp	lemon grass powder	1/2	tsp	chili sauce
1	medium	carrot, thinly sliced			

Procedure

1. In a large saucepan, heat 1/2 cup broth over medium heat. Add the shallot, garlic, and lemon grass and sauté for 2 min. Add the carrot and mushrooms and sauté for 3 min.

2. Add the remaining 4 cups broth and bring to a boil. Lower the heat and simmer for 20 min. In a small bowl, combine the Bragg's, sherry, and chili puree. Add to the soup and simmer for 3 more min.

Servings: 4

Preparation Time: 10 minutes
Cooking Time: 30 minutes

Nutrition Facts

Serving size: 1/4 of a recipe (11.6 ounces).

Amount Per Serving	
Calories	99.01
Calories From Fat (3%)	2.77
	% Daily Value
Total Fat 0.33g	<1%
Saturated Fat 0.07g	<1%
Cholesterol 0mg	0%
Sodium 636.05mg	27%
Potassium 466.96mg	13%
Total Carbohydrates 23.95g	8%
Fiber 2.59g	10%
Sugar 3.39g	
Protein 2.36g	5%

Lentil Soup

1		onion chopped	1	(14.5 oz)	can crushed tomatoes
1/4 cup		olive oil			
2		carrots, diced	2	cups	dry lentils, rinsed
2		Stalks celery chopped	8	cups	water
2	cloves	garlic clove, minced	1/2 cup		spinach rinsed and thinly sliced
1	tsp	dried oregano			
1		bay leaf	2	Tbsp	vinegar
1	tsp	dried basil	½	tsp	salt
			½	tsp	black pepper

Procedure

1. In a large soup pot, heat oil over medium heat. Add onions, carrots, and celery; cook and stir until onion is tender. Stir in garlic, bay leaf, oregano, and basil; cook for 2 minutes.

2. Stir in lentils, and add water and tomatoes. Bring to a boil. Reduce heat, and simmer for at least 1 hour. Stir in spinach, and cook until it wilts. Stir in vinegar, and salt and pepper.

Servings: 6
Yield: 6

Nutrition Facts

Serving size: 1/6 of a recipe (18.6 ounces).

Amount Per Serving	
Calories	342.7
Calories From Fat (26%)	87.53
	% Daily Value
Total Fat 9.92g	15%
Saturated Fat 1.39g	7%
Cholesterol 0mg	0%
Sodium 190.42mg	8%
Potassium 927.97mg	27%
Total Carbohydrates 47.13g	16%
Fiber 21.83g	87%
Sugar 5.33g	
Protein 17.83g	36%

Louisiana Gumbo

2	Tbsp	butter	1		spring fresh thyme
3		cloves garlic minced	2		bay leaves
			1	pinch	salt
2	cups	chopped onion	1/2	tsp	ground cayenne pepper
3/4	cup	chopped celery	1	pinch	ground black pepper
1	pound	okra chopped	1	pound	andouille , sausage cut into 1/2 inch pieces
1/4	cup	butter			
1/4	cup	rice flour	1/2	pound	crabmeat, flaked
1/2	pound	cubed beef stew meat	1	pound	medium shrimp, peeled and deveined
8	cups	water	1/2	tsp	hot pepper sauce
1	(16 oz) can	chopped tomatoes	1/4	cup	Worcestershire sauce
			1/2		lemon, juice
1 1/2	tsp	agave nectar			file powder (lightly sprinkled, per bowl)
1 1/2	Tbsp	chopped fresh parsley			

Procedure

1. Melt butter in a large skillet over medium heat. Cook garlic, onions, celery and okra, stirring constantly until golden brown. Set aside.

2. In a large heavy bottomed stock pot over medium-high heat, combine butter and flour. Cook, stirring constantly, until the roux becomes chocolate brown. Stir in the vegetable mixture, and stew meat. Cook, stirring over medium-low, until vegetables are tender, and meat is evenly brown. Stir in water, tomatoes and agave. Season with parsley, thyme, bay leaves, salt, cayenne pepper and black pepper. Bring to a boil, reduce heat, and simmer for 2 1/2 hours, stirring occasionally.

3. Add shrimp, crabmeat and andouille to stock pot. Stir in hot pepper sauce, Worcestershire sauce and lemon. Simmer an additional 10 minutes, stirring occasionally. Remove bay leaves, sprinkle with file powder, and serve.

Servings: 10

Yield: 10

Preparation Time: 30 minutes
Cooking Time: 3 hours and 30 minutes
Total Time: 4 hours

Nutrition Facts

Serving size: 1/10 of a recipe (15.8 ounces).

Amount Per Serving	
Calories	202.45
Calories From Fat (48%)	96.56
	% Daily Value
Total Fat 10.9g	17%
Saturated Fat 5.58g	28%
Cholesterol 88.76mg	30%
Sodium 678.43mg	28%
Potassium 493.71mg	14%
Total Carbohydrates 15.16g	5%
Fiber 2.87g	11%
Sugar 6.07g	
Protein 11.94g	24%

Mulligatawny

1/2	cup	chopped onion	1/2		apple cored and chopped
2	stalks	celery chopped	1/4 cup		white rice uncooked
1		carrot diced	1		skinless, boneless chicken breast half cut into cubes
1/4	cup	butter			salt to taste
1 1/2	Tbsp	all purpose flour			ground black pepper to taste
1 1/2	tsp	curry powder	1	pinch	dried thyme
4	cups	chicken broth	1/2 cup		heavy cream, heated

Procedure

1. Sauté onions, celery, carrot, and butter in a large soup pot. Add flour and curry, and cook 5 more minutes. Add chicken broth, mix well, and bring to a boil. Simmer 30 minutes.
2. Add apple, rice, chicken, salt, pepper, and thyme. Simmer 15-20 minutes, or until rice is done. Remove from heat.
3. Add hot cream and stir.

Servings: 6
Yield: 6

Preparation Time: 20 minutes
Cooking Time: 1 hour
Total Time: 1 hour

Nutrition Facts

Serving size: 1/6 of a recipe (9.4 ounces).

Amount Per Serving	
Calories	242.02
Calories From Fat (61%)	147.29
	% Daily Value
Total Fat 16.67g	26%
Saturated Fat 9.88g	49%
Cholesterol 59.69mg	20%
Sodium 579.91mg	24%
Potassium 326.04mg	9%
Total Carbohydrates 13.79g	5%
Fiber 1.48g	6%
Sugar 3.19g	
Protein 9.4g	19%

Pasta Fagioli

3	Tbsp	olive oil	1 1/2	tsp	dried oregano
1		onion	1	tsp	salt
		quartered and halved	1	(15 oz) can	cannellini beans
2	cloves	garlic minced	1	(15 oz) can	navy beans
1	(29 oz) can	tomato sauce	1/3	cup	grated Parmesan cheese
5 1/2	cup	water			
1	Tbsp	dried parsley			
1 1/2	tsp	dried basil	1/2	pound	ditalini pasta, wholegrain

Procedure

1 In a large pot over medium heat, cook onion in olive oil until translucent. Stir in garlic and cook until tender. Reduce heat, and stir in tomato sauce, water, parsley, basil, oregano, salt, cannellini beans, navy beans and Parmesan. Simmer 1 hour.

2 Bring a large pot of lightly salted water to a boil. Add pasta and cook for 8 to 10 minutes or until al dente; drain. Stir into soup.

Servings: 8
Yield: 8

Preparation Time: 10 minutes
Cooking Time: 1 hour and 30 minutes
Total Time: 1 hour and 40 minutes

Nutrition Facts

Serving size: 1/8 of a recipe (11.6 ounces).

Amount Per Serving	
Calories	250.5
Calories From Fat (24%)	61.19
	% Daily Value
Total Fat 6.96g	**11%**
Saturated Fat 1.54g	**8%**
Cholesterol 3.66mg	**1%**
Sodium 526.41mg	**22%**
Potassium 908.05mg	**26%**
Total Carbohydrates 34.85g	**12%**
Fiber 11.15g	**45%**
Sugar 3.02g	
Protein 14.02g	**28%**

Cream of Tomato Basil Soup

4		tomatoes peeled, seeded and diced
4	cups	tomato juice
14		leaves fresh basil
1/2 cup		milk

1/2 cup heavy whipping cream

1/2 cup butter

salt and pepper to taste

Procedure

1 Place tomatoes and juice in a stock pot over medium heat. Simmer for 30 minutes. Puree the tomato mixture along with the basil leaves, and return the puree to the stock pot.

2 Place the pot over medium heat, and stir in the milk, heavy cream and butter. Season with salt and pepper. Heat, stirring until the butter is melted. Do not boil.

Servings: 4
Yield: 4

Preparation Time: 10 minutes
Cooking Time: 35 minutes
Total Time: 45 minutes

Nutrition Facts

Serving size: 1/4 of a recipe (17.7 ounces).

Amount Per Serving	
Calories	428.41
Calories From Fat (73%)	313.54
	% Daily Value
Total Fat 35.7g	55%
Saturated Fat 22.21g	111%
Cholesterol 104.2mg	35%
Sodium 115.22mg	5%
Potassium 1393.06mg	40%
Total Carbohydrates 26.51g	9%
Fiber 8.75g	35%
Sugar 14.87g	
Protein 8.68g	17%

Slow-Cooker Chicken Tortilla Soup

1	pound	shredded cooked chicken	1	tsp	salt
			1/4	tsp	black pepper
1	(15 oz) can	Rotel diced tomatoes with habanero	1		bay leaf
			1	(10 oz) package	frozen corn
1	(10 oz) can	enchilada sauce	1	can (15 oz)	black beans
1	medium	onion chopped	1	Tbsp	chopped cilantro
1	(4 ounce) can	chopped green chili peppers	7		corn tortillas
					vegetable oil
2	cloves	garlic minced	1	cup	cheese, grated Mexican
2	cups	water			
1	(14.5 oz) can	chicken broth			
2	tsp	cumin	1		avocado diced
1	tsp	chili powder			

Procedure

1. Place chicken, tomatoes, enchilada sauce, onion, green chilies, and garlic into a slow cooker. Pour in water and chicken broth, and season with cumin, chili powder, salt, pepper, and bay leaf. Stir in corn and cilantro. Cover, and cook on Low setting for 6 to 8 hours or on High setting for 3 to 4 hours.
2. Preheat oven to 400 degrees F (200 degrees C).
3. Lightly brush both sides of tortillas with oil. Cut tortillas into strips, and then spread on a baking sheet.
4. Bake in preheated oven until crisp, about 10 to 15 minutes. To serve, sprinkle cheese, tortilla strips and avocado over soup.

Servings: 8

Preparation Time: 30 minutes
Cooking Time: 8 hours
Total Time: 8 hours and 30 minutes

Nutrition Facts

Serving size: 1/8 of a recipe (12.3 ounces).

Amount Per Serving	
Calories	306.15
Calories From Fat (31%)	96.14
	% Daily Value
Total Fat 11.03g	17%
Saturated Fat 2.85g	14%
Cholesterol 55.95mg	19%
Sodium 853.2mg	36%
Potassium 613.87mg	18%
Total Carbohydrates 26.7g	9%
Fiber 6.14g	25%
Sugar 2.81g	
Protein 26.7g	53%

Southwest Soup

1	cup	mixed vegetables [peppers, onions, carrots etc]	1	Tbsp	chili powder
			1/4	tsp	garlic powder
			1/4	tsp	salt
			1/4	tsp	oregano
1	can (15 oz)	chopped tomatoes	1	pinch	cumin seeds
1	can (15 oz)	black beans	2		chicken breasts, chopped
2	cups	water			
1	tsp	vegetable bouillon			
1/8	tsp	black pepper			
1/8	tsp	cayenne pepper			

Procedure

1 Combine ingredients in a slow cooker and cook for 4 hours on "High."

Servings: 8
Yield: 8

Nutrition Facts

Serving size: 1/8 of a recipe (10.5 ounces).

Amount Per Serving	
Calories	153.62
Calories From Fat (13%)	19.78
	% Daily Value
Total Fat 2.26g	3%
Saturated Fat 0.47g	2%
Cholesterol 37.78mg	13%
Sodium 391.63mg	16%
Potassium 627.8mg	18%
Total Carbohydrates 17.55g	6%
Fiber 5.55g	22%
Sugar 2.44g	
Protein 17.31g	35%

Squash Bisque

4 1/2 cup	winter squash, peeled, seeded and cubed into ¼" chunks		1 1/2 tsp	ground cumin	
			1/4 tsp	ground nutmeg	
			1/4 tsp	cayenne pepper or to taste	
1	cup	chopped onion	1	tsp	salt
3 1/4 cup	vegetable broth		1/4 cup	sour cream	
2	cloves	garlic, minced			
1	tsp	ground cardamom			

Procedure

1. Preheat the oven to 375°F.
2. Place squash in a baking dish and bake for 30 min. or until tender. Set aside.
3. In a large stock pot, sauté the onion 1/4 cup broth over medium heat until translucent, about 3 min. Add garlic, cardamom, cumin, nutmeg, cayenne and salt. Sauté for 2 to 3 min. Put in the cooked squash. Add the remaining 3 cups broth.
4. Puree the soup in batches in a food processor or blender until smooth.
5. Return soup to pot and bring to a boil. Turn down to simmer, partially cover pot, and simmer for 10 min or until heated thoroughly.
6. Garnish the top of each bowl of soup with 1 tbsp sour cream.

Servings: 6
Yield: 6

Preparation Time: 30 minutes
Cooking Time: 50 minutes

Nutrition Facts

Serving size: 1/6 of a recipe (10.3 ounces).

Amount Per Serving	
Calories	96.22
Calories From Fat (6%)	6.14
	% Daily Value
Total Fat 0.7g	1%
Saturated Fat 0.31g	2%
Cholesterol 2.64mg	<1%
Sodium 713mg	30%
Potassium 491.89mg	14%
Total Carbohydrates 21.71g	7%
Fiber 2.76g	11%
Sugar 6.69g	
Protein 2.93g	6%

Spicy Chicken Soup

2	quarts	water	3	cloves	garlic chopped
8		skinless, boneless chicken breast halves	1	(16 oz) jar	chunky salsa
1/2	tsp	salt	2	(14.5 oz) can	peeled and diced tomatoes
1	tsp	ground black pepper			
1	tsp	garlic powder	1	(14.5 oz) can	whole peeled tomatoes
2	Tbsp	dried parsley			
1	Tbsp	onion powder	1	(10.75 oz) can	diced tomatoes
5	cubes	chicken bouillon			
3	Tbsp	olive oil	3	Tbsp	chili powder
1		onion chopped	1	(15 oz) can	whole kernel corn drained
			2	(16 oz) can	chili beans, undrained
			1	(8 oz) container	sour cream

Procedure

1. In a large pot over medium heat, combine water, chicken, salt, pepper, garlic powder, parsley, onion powder and bouillon cubes. Bring to a boil, then reduce heat and simmer 1 hour, or until chicken juices run clear. Remove chicken, reserve broth. Shred chicken.

2. In a large pot over medium heat, cook onion and garlic in olive oil until slightly browned. Stir in salsa, diced tomatoes, whole tomatoes, tomatoes, chili powder, corn, chili beans, sour cream, shredded chicken and 5 cups broth. Simmer 30 minutes.

Servings: 8
Yield: 8

Preparation Time: 15 minutes
Cooking Time: 30 minutes
Total Time: 45 minutes

Nutrition Facts

Serving size: 1/8 of a recipe (28.6 ounces).

Amount Per Serving	
Calories	565.02
Calories From Fat (38%)	216.16
	% Daily Value
Total Fat 24.29g	37%
Saturated Fat 8.26g	41%
Cholesterol 180.23mg	60%
Sodium 1997.08mg	83%
Potassium 1641.62mg	47%
Total Carbohydrates 28.3g	9%
Fiber 5.19g	21%
Sugar 9.1g	
Protein 58.64g	117%

Vegetable, Fruit and Lentil Soup

1/4 cup	butter		1/2 tsp	ground black pepper
2	large sweet potatoes peeled and chopped into ¼ inch cubes		1 tsp	salt
			1/2 tsp	ground cumin
			1/2 tsp	chili powder
3	large carrot peeled and chopped		1/2 tsp	paprika
			4 cups	vegetable broth
1	apple peeled, cored and chopped			plain yogurt
1	onion chopped			
1/2 cup	red lentils			
1/2 tsp	minced fresh ginger			

Procedure

1 Melt the butter in a large, heavy bottomed pot over medium-high heat. Place the chopped sweet potatoes, carrots, apple, and onion in the pot. Stir and cook the apples and vegetables until the onions are translucent, about 10 minutes.

2 Stir the lentils, ginger, ground black pepper, salt, cumin, chili powder, paprika, and vegetable broth into the pot with the apple and vegetable mixture. Bring the soup to a boil over high heat, and then reduce the heat to medium-low, cover, and simmer until the lentils and vegetables are soft, about 30 minutes.

3 Puree the soup with a hand blender.

4 Continue simmering over medium-high heat, about 10 minutes. Add water as needed to thin the soup to your preferred consistency. Serve with yogurt for garnish.

Servings: 6
Yield: 6

Preparation Time: 20 minutes
Cooking Time: 50 minutes
Total Time: 1 hour and 10 minutes

Nutrition Facts

Serving size: 1/6 of a recipe (12.3 ounces).

Amount Per Serving	
Calories	284.94
Calories From Fat (35%)	98.44
	% Daily Value
Total Fat 11.17g	17%
Saturated Fat 5.91g	30%
Cholesterol 24.43mg	8%
Sodium 1558.9mg	65%
Potassium 720.74mg	21%
Total Carbohydrates 39.95g	13%
Fiber 5.67g	23%
Sugar 9.91g	
Protein 8.22g	16%

Vegetarian Tortilla Soup

2	Tbsp	vegetable oil	½ tsp ea.		Salt and pepper
1	pound	package frozen pepper and onion stir fry mix	1 can	11-oz	whole kernel corn
			12	ounces	tortilla chips
			1	cup	shredded Cheddar cheese
2		garlic clove, minced	1		avocado peeled, pitted and diced
3	Tbsp	ground cumin			
1 can	2 cups	crushed tomatoes with chili peppers			
3 cans	4 ounce	chopped green chili peppers, drained			
4 cans	14 ounce	vegetable broth			

Procedure

Heat the oil in a large pot over medium heat. Stir in the pepper and onion stir fry mix, garlic, and cumin, and cook 5 minutes, until vegetables are tender. Mix in the tomatoes and chili peppers. Pour in the broth, and salt and pepper. Bring to a boil, reduce heat to low, and simmer 30 minutes.

Servings: 12
Yield: 12

Preparation Time: 15 minutes
Cooking Time: 40 minutes
Total Time: 55 minutes

Nutrition Facts

Serving size: 1/12 of a recipe (2 ounces).

Amount Per Serving	
Calories	315
Calories From Fat (44%)	139.43
	% Daily Value
Total Fat 16.2g	**25%**
Saturated Fat 4g	**20%**
Cholesterol 12mg	**4%**
Sodium 1152mg	**48%**
Potassium 461mg	**13%**
Total Carbohydrates 37.2g	**12%**
Fiber 5.9g	**24%**
Sugar 3.9g	
Protein 8.7g	**17%**

Made in the USA
Lexington, KY
25 April 2013